Gooseberry Patch Co.
get-togethers
WITH GOOSEBERRY PATCH

A heartfelt "thanks"... to each & every one of you who helped make this book a reality. And to our families, thank you for your love and encouragement.

With food that brings family & friends to the table, and ideas for celebrating in new ways, we hope this book is an inspiration for many fun-filled get-togethers!

 1-931890-62-5
First Printing, May, 2005

1-800-854-6673
www.gooseberrypatch.com

Vickie & Jo Ann

THE GOOSEBERRY PATCH STORY

As friends and neighbors we'd taken many evening walks together chatting about our kids, an upcoming auction or making plans for a road trip to the next flea market. We both loved country style and vintage finds, and it was during one walk home in the fall of 1984 that the idea for a mail-order company came about.

We loved the thought of working from home and being with our families, and after several brainstorming sessions at the kitchen table, we created our very first catalog! We filled our catalog to the brim with country favorites like quilts, handmade cookie cutters, baskets, candles and wreaths, and soon we began receiving letters from customers who had become like friends to us. It wasn't long before they began sharing tried & true recipes, traditions, tips and ideas. So, in 1992, we gathered together their handed-down recipes and heart-felt holiday memories, combined them with whimsical illustrations and created a cookbook called ***Old-Fashioned Country Christmas***. Since then, we've created more than 50 community-style cookbooks.

Gooseberry Patch is also a lifestyle, where time spent with those we love means the most. And in ***Get-Togethers with Gooseberry Patch***, our very first full-color book, we're excited to share fresh, fun, easy ideas for bringing everyone together. Also inside are some of our very best recipes, each one tested, that you'll find yourself wanting to make again & again.

Life's all about celebrating the little things...a picnic in the country, a trip to the farmers' market, brisk autumn days, the crunch of snow underfoot and sweet holiday homecomings. Each season has its own special moments, and no matter where we find ourselves, sharing those moments always brings love and laughter to our hearts.

So come along! With this many simple country pleasures to be found, there's no better time than now to bring food, family & friends together!

Enjoy every moment!
Vickie & JoAnn

1895
LORINA
SPARKLING

contents

Spring's sprouting...

a fragrant breeze, snowdrops and daffodils, the sound of a gentle rain. Spring is worth waiting for and there's no better time to plant the seeds for a gardening get-together.

Keep the menu a breeze...Sun-Dried Tomato & Parmesan Quiche and Fresh Spinach Salad with Strawberries are perfect paired with tall glasses of ice-cold Minted Mango Tea. For a sweet & simple dessert, Bursting with Berries Bundt Cake is filled with plump, juicy berries and topped with a dusting of powdered sugar.

After lunch, friends can slip on gardening gloves and aprons and begin potting up perennials brought from home to share...what a terrific way to start a Friendship Garden. Swapping plants will be a sweet reminder of this day spent together. It's time to sing out spring!

garden lunch

- COOL-AS-A-CUCUMBER SOUP
- ORANGE-MELON SUNSHINE SALAD
- FRESH SPINACH SALAD WITH STRAWBERRIES
- TARRAGON-PARSLEY BUTTER
- DILLY EGG SALAD ON PUMPERNICKEL
- SPICED ZUCCHINI BREAD
- SUN-DRIED TOMATO & PARMESAN QUICHE
- CHUNKY CHICKEN SALAD WITH SMOKED GOUDA
- ITALIAN BEAN SALAD WITH TUNA
- BURSTING WITH BERRIES BUNDT CAKE
- MINTED MANGO TEA

garden

Cool-as-a-Cucumber Soup

Made with half-and-half, this chilled soup is unbelievably creamy...be sure to keep second helpings on hand!

4 cucumbers, chopped
1/2 c. fresh mint, torn
1 t. fresh dill, chopped
1 cube chicken bouillon
1/4 c. hot water
1 c. half-and-half
salt to taste
3 to 4 t. sugar
Garnish: sour cream, fresh mint sprigs

Blend all ingredients except garnish in a blender in small batches. Whisk together; taste and add more salt or sugar, if necessary. Chill for at least 2 hours. When ready to serve, whisk briefly before spooning into bowls. Top each bowl with a dollop of sour cream and a sprig of mint. Serves 4 to 6.

Orange-Melon Sunshine Salad

Mad over melon? Try adding honeydew, cantaloupe or even watermelon to this refreshing fruit salad!

2 c. orange juice
2 slices fresh ginger root
4 to 6 c. mixed melon balls
Garnish: fresh mint sprigs

Bring orange juice and ginger slices to a boil in a medium saucepan over medium heat. Continue to boil until juice reduces to 1/2 to 3/4 of its original amount. Remove from heat and discard ginger slices. Let cool. Arrange fruit in a shallow pan; pour juice over top. Chill for 2 hours to overnight. Place fruit in a serving bowl; pour juice over the top and garnish with mint. Serves 4 to 6.

lunch

Fresh Spinach Salad with Strawberries

Bursting with flavor, the pairing of the tangy dressing and sweet summer strawberries is simply divine.

1/2 c. sugar
1/2 c. olive oil
1/4 c. vinegar
2 T. sesame seed
1 T. poppy seed
1 T. dried, minced onion
1/4 t. paprika
1/4 t. Worcestershire sauce
10-oz. pkg. spinach, rinsed and torn into bite-size pieces
1 qt. strawberries, hulled and sliced
1/4 c. blanched, slivered almonds

Whisk together sugar, oil, vinegar, sesame seed, poppy seed, onion, paprika and Worcestershire sauce in a medium bowl. Cover and chill for one hour. Combine spinach, strawberries and almonds in a large bowl; pour dressing over salad and toss. Refrigerate 10 to 15 minutes before serving. Serves 4.

Tarragon-Parsley Butter

Personalize this butter with your favorite herb blend...try oregano with minced garlic or rosemary and thyme!

1/2 c. butter
1 t. fresh tarragon, chopped
1 t. fresh parsley, chopped
1 t. onion, minced

Whisk butter just until softened. Add herbs and onion; blend in well. Form into a roll on plastic wrap; chill. To serve, cut into 1/2-inch slices. Makes 1/2 cup.

Remember those delicate teacups you found for a song at that estate sale? They're just right for serving salads, soup and even dessert to extra-special guests. Perfect for potting up seedlings to take home too!

Dilly Egg Salad on Pumpernickel

The combination of red onion, dill and Dijon makes this lunchtime favorite extra special.

8 eggs
2 T. mayonnaise
2 T. Dijon mustard
1 t. dill weed
1/2 t. paprika
1/3 c. red onion, minced
salt and pepper to taste
8 slices pumpernickel bread

Place eggs in a large saucepan; cover with cold water and bring to a boil. Boil for 10 to 12 minutes; remove from heat. Run eggs under cold water until cool enough to handle; peel and chop. Place eggs and remaining ingredients except pumpernickel bread in a large bowl; mash well with a fork or wooden spoon. Serve on pumpernickel bread or over lettuce. Makes 4 servings.

Spiced Zucchini Bread

With a swoop of cream cheese on top, this bread will disappear in a flash.

15.4-oz. pkg. nut bread mix
1 egg
1 t. pumpkin pie spice
2/3 c. milk
2 T. oil
1 c. zucchini, shredded

Combine all ingredients except zucchini in a bowl; mix until well blended. Fold in zucchini. Pour into a 9"x5" loaf pan that has been greased on the bottom only. Bake at 350 degrees for 45 to 55 minutes, or until a toothpick inserted in the center comes out clean. Makes one loaf.

Look for vintage-style seed packets next time you're at the flea market or garden store. Cut a small hole in the top and bottom and thread onto short twigs. Poke down into tiny terra cotta pots and hold in place with a little potting soil. They'll make great place markers or, when grouped together, a clever centerpiece!

Try topping cupcakes or fruit salad with edible flowers at your garden lunch. Most taste just like their scent, with just a touch of sweetness.

Here are some of our favorites:

impatiens
pansies
nasturtium
lilacs
rose petals
violets
snapdragons

Be sure to select pesticide-free blooms or those from your own garden.

Hosting a Plant Swap

Daisies and daylilies always seem to sprout up faster than we can count them while summertime herbs multiply quicker than the days fly by.

Share the wealth with some good friends and host a plant swap! All you need are a few seedlings to trade, some fellow garden buffs and a picnic table in a shady spot.

The more, the merrier...everyone just brings at least as many plants as they'd like to take home. Set them all out on the table and trade away!

Be sure to have a few creative containers on hand to separate any blooms. We've made a list of our favorites below to inspire you.

The best part (besides the visiting with friends, of course!) is chatting with the gal who brought your plant to swap. She'll know what kind of light and how much water it likes...what a terrific trade-off!

A fun and relaxing way to spend an afternoon with friends in the sunshine...with bountiful rewards!

Creative Container Ideas

vintage teacups
paper take-out boxes
paper lunch bags
berry buckets
galvanized pails
pressed glass jelly jars
enamelware mugs
muffin tins
vintage measuring cups
custard cups

garden

Sun-Dried Tomato & Parmesan Quiche

Add mushrooms, broccoli, carrots or even eggplant in place of the zucchini...as long as it adds up to 5 cups, the possibilities are endless!

10-inch pie crust
2 T. butter
1/2 c. shallots, diced
1 clove garlic, finely minced
5 c. zucchini, thinly sliced
salt and pepper to taste
1/2 lb. deli ham, finely diced
5 eggs, beaten
1/3 c. sun-dried tomatoes packed in oil, drained and chopped
3/4 c. milk
1/2 c. whipping cream
1/4 c. grated Parmesan cheese
paprika to taste

Place pie crust in a 10" pie plate; line with foil. Weight with pie weights or dried beans and bake at 350 degrees for 20 minutes. Remove weights and foil from crust; set aside. Melt butter in a large skillet over medium-high heat: add shallots and garlic. Sauté for about 3 minutes, until transparent. Add zucchini and salt and pepper to taste; cook for about 5 minutes, stirring gently. Drain well. Add ham and remove from heat; set aside. Combine eggs, tomatoes, milk, cream, and salt and pepper to taste in a separate bowl; add to zucchini mixture. Pour into crust and sprinkle with Parmesan. Cover top edge of crust with a strip of aluminum foil. Increase oven to 375 degrees; place quiche on a baking sheet and bake for 30 minutes. Reduce oven to 350 degrees; sprinkle quiche with paprika and bake for an additional 15 minutes. Serves 6 to 8.

lunch

Chunky Chicken Salad with Smoked Gouda

Serve on a bed of fresh spinach leaves and garnish with fresh herbs!

3/4 lb. boneless, skinless chicken breast
1/8 t. salt
1/4 t. pepper
8 c. spinach, torn
3/4 c. red pepper, chopped
1/2 c. celery, thinly sliced
1/2 c. red onion, sliced and separated into rings
1-1/2 c. Red Delicious apple, cored and thinly sliced
3/4 c. honey-mustard salad dressing
1/2 c. smoked Gouda or Jarlsberg cheese, shredded
1/4 c. sliced almonds, toasted

Sprinkle chicken with salt and pepper. Arrange on a broiler pan coated with non-stick vegetable spray; broil 5 minutes on each side or until juices run clear. Let cool; cut chicken into 1/4-inch thick slices. Combine chicken, spinach, red pepper, celery, onion and apple in a large bowl. Drizzle dressing over salad and toss well; sprinkle with cheese and almonds. Serves 6.

Italian Bean Salad with Tuna

Cannellini beans make this light salad hearty enough for a main dish.

12-oz. can white albacore tuna, drained
2 15-oz. cans cannellini beans, drained and rinsed
1/3 c. capers, rinsed
3/4 c. olive oil
6 T. red wine vinegar
salt and pepper to taste
1-1/2 c. cherry tomatoes, halved
1 red onion, thinly sliced
Garnish: 1 T. fresh basil, chopped

Combine tuna, beans and capers in a large bowl; set aside. Whisk together oil and vinegar; add salt and pepper to taste. Pour dressing over tuna mixture; add tomatoes and onion and toss lightly. Serve immediately, garnished with fresh basil. Makes 4 to 6 servings.

Bursting with Berries Bundt Cake

Try it with black raspberries, huckleberries, cherries or even gooseberries!

5 eggs
1-2/3 c. sugar
1-1/4 c. unsalted butter, diced and softened
2 T. kirsch liqueur or blackberry syrup
1 t. baking powder
1/8 t. salt
2-1/2 c. all-purpose flour, divided
1-1/2 c. raspberries
1-1/2 c. blueberries or blackberries
Garnish: powdered sugar

Combine eggs and sugar in a large bowl; set aside. Beat butter and liqueur or syrup until fluffy using an electric mixer; add to egg mixture. Add baking powder, salt and all except 2 tablespoons flour. Beat until well-blended and no lumps remain; set aside. Combine berries and remaining flour; toss to coat berries. Gently fold berries into batter. Pour into a greased and floured Bundt® pan. Bake at 325 degrees until a wooden pick inserted into center comes out clean, about one hour. Remove from oven and let cool in the pan for 20 to 25 minutes; turn out onto a wire rack to cool completely. Sprinkle top of cake with powdered sugar. Serves 10 to 12.

Minted Mango Tea

Oh my, mango! It's a tasty twist on our refreshment of choice.

1 c. mango slices, chopped
1 c. pineapple juice
4 c. boiling water
8 green teabags
2 fresh mint sprigs
1 to 2 T. sugar
ice cubes to taste
Garnish: mango slices

Blend mango and pineapple juice in a blender, covered, until smooth; chill and set aside. Place teabags and mint sprigs in a large glass bowl; pour boiling water over top and let steep 5 minutes. Remove and discard teabags and mint sprigs. Chill, covered, for 2 to 3 hours. Transfer to a 2-quart pitcher; add puréed mango mixture and sugar. Stir until sugar is dissolved. Pour into ice-filled glasses; garnish each glass with a mango slice. Makes 6 servings.

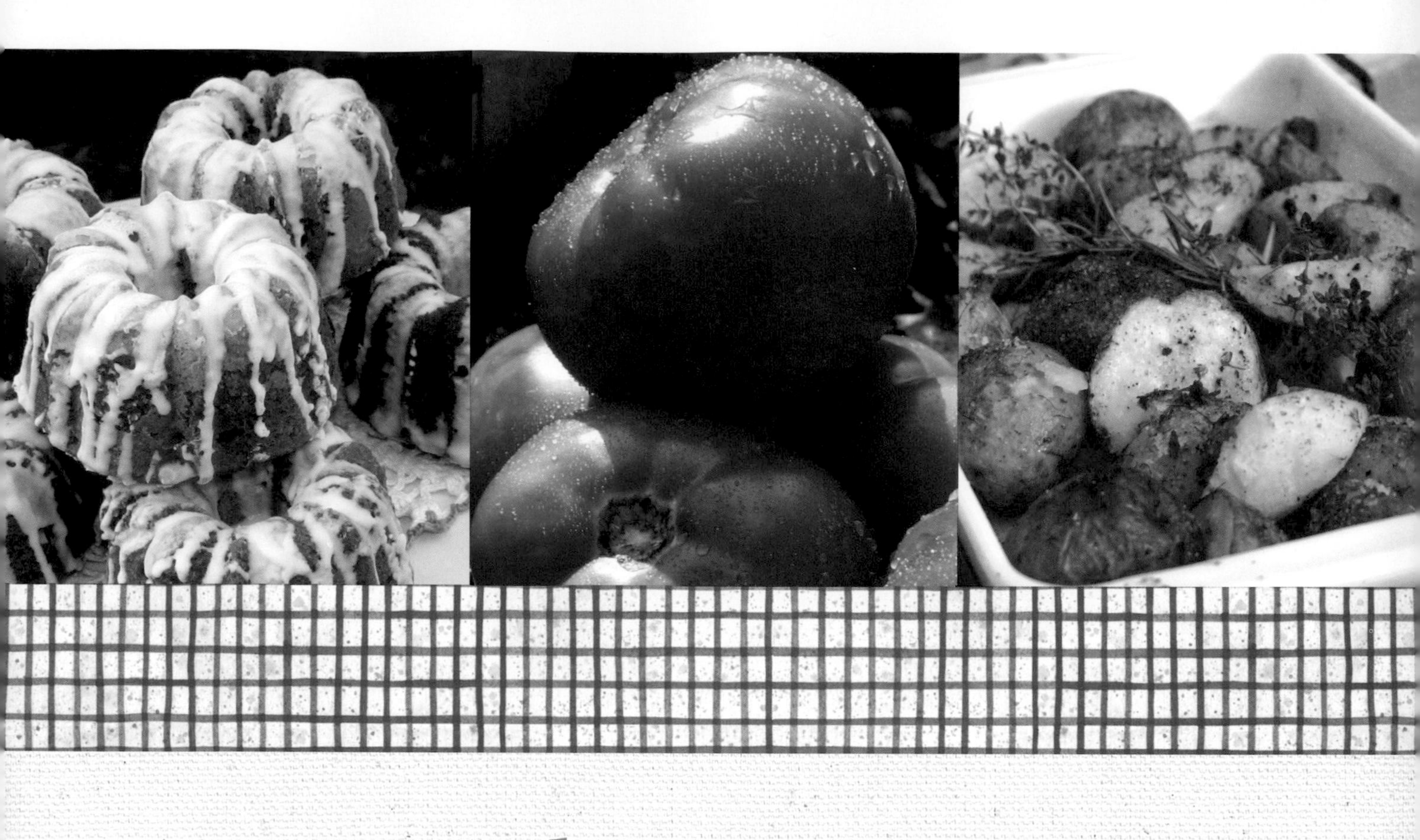

Ah, summer...

long, sun-drenched days, family picnics, spirited parades and we all know there's nothing finer than a juicy tomato still warm from the summer sun. We think one of the best things about summer is heading out to a farmers' market. Crisp, crunchy vegetables alongside baskets bursting with ripe berries...definitely something to crow about!

Fruits & vegetables plucked right from the garden make mealtime fuss free. Try serving Chunky Corn & Tomato Gazpacho from a chilled canning jar...what a clever soup tureen as well as a tasty hot-weather soup. And a slice of Triple Cheese Tart alongside Creamy Cucumber Crunch is one of summertime's best dinners. Ready for dessert? Then it's time to pour a frosty glass of Sweet Tea with Lemon and linger over warm Old-Fashioned Black Raspberry Buckle.

Simple, country-style food is always just right. And whether you're picnicking under a shady tree or with family & friends gathered 'round the table, it's sure to be a part of bringing everyone together.

farmers' market

CHUNKY CORN & TOMATO GAZPACHO

SWEET-AS-SUGAR SNAP PEAS

TRIPLE CHEESE TART

CREAMY CUCUMBER CRUNCH

HERB ROASTED POTATOES

BROCCO-FLOWER SALAD

MINI CARROT BUNDT CAKES

OLD-FASHIONED BLACK RASPBERRY BUCKLE

JUST PEACHY HAND PIES

SWEET TEA WITH LEMON

SUMMERTIME BERRY SMOOTHIE

Chunky Corn & Tomato Gazpacho

This chilled soup is so refreshing after a day in the sunshine...use your fresh veggie finds from the market.

1 c. corn, cooked
2 yellow tomatoes, seeded and chopped
3 c. tomato juice
1 cucumber, diced
1/2 c. onion, minced
1/4 t. chili powder
1 clove garlic, minced
2 T. fresh basil, chopped
3 T. lime juice
1/2 t. salt
1/4 t. pepper
Garnish: fresh basil sprigs

Combine all ingredients in a bowl; mix well. Chill for one hour before serving. Serves 6.

Sweet-as-Sugar Snap Peas

The sweetness of the snap peas is perfect with just a touch of tanginess from the red onion...delicious!

1 lb. sugar snap peas
1/2 c. red onion, thinly sliced
2 cloves garlic, minced
2 T. olive oil
1/2 t. salt
1/4 t. pepper

Cover peas with water in a large saucepan and boil for 3 minutes; drain and rinse with cold water. Combine all ingredients; toss to coat. Cover and chill for one hour to overnight. Serves 4.

Triple Cheese Tart

Triple the cheese? It must be triple yummy too!

1-1/2 c. all-purpose flour
1/2 c. butter
5 to 6 T. cold water
1/2 c. pecan pieces, toasted
2 3-oz. pkgs. cream cheese, softened
1/2 c. half-and-half
2 eggs, beaten
1/2 c. crumbled blue cheese
1/3 c. sun-dried tomatoes packed in oil, drained and chopped
1/4 c. green onion, chopped
1/2 c. shredded Swiss cheese
1 t. Worcestershire sauce
Garnish: chopped fresh chives

Place flour in a small bowl; cut in butter and mix until crumbly. Stir in water until moistened; shape into a ball. Roll out onto a lightly floured surface into a 14-inch circle. Place into a greased 11" round tart pan with a removable bottom. Press dough onto bottom and up sides of pan; cut away extra dough and prick all over with fork. Bake at 400 degrees for 16 to 18 minutes or until golden. Place pecans on bottom of crust; set aside.

Beat cream cheese at medium speed in a large mixing bowl for one to 2 minutes until creamy. Add half-and-half and eggs; mix well. Stir in blue cheese, tomatoes, onion, Swiss cheese and Worcestershire sauce. Pour into crust; bake at 350 degrees for 30 to 35 minutes or until knife inserted near center comes out clean. Cut into wedges; garnish with chives, if desired. Serves 10 to 12.

Sweet herbal sugar couldn't be simpler to make and looks lovely in a vintage sugar bowl or glass jar. Pick fresh rosemary or lavender blossoms, grind with sugar and store in an airtight jar...add a few fresh sprigs to intensify the flavor. Stir into cake or cookie mixes, a cup of tea or even salad dressing!

Summertime is the prime time for farmers' markets. As soon as the weather warms, keep an eye out for notices announcing open-air markets in your area. Be sure to dress comfortably, take cash along and keep your shopping list flexible. The best part about shopping fresh markets is finding something you'd never find at the supermarket, like heirloom varieties of tomatoes, homemade jellies and homebaked bread.

Creamy Cucumber Crunch

With a dreamy dressing and the satisfying crunch of fresh veggies, this salad is always a hit at gatherings.

8 cucumbers
1 t. salt
6 radishes, thinly sliced
8-oz. container plain yogurt
1/2 c. sour cream
1/2 c. fresh dill, chopped and loosely packed
2 T. lime juice
1/4 t. pepper
1 clove garlic, pressed

Remove several strips of peel from each cucumber; cut in half lengthwise. Scoop out seeds and slice each half thinly crosswise. Toss cucumbers with salt in a large bowl; set aside for 30 minutes. Combine radishes, yogurt, sour cream, dill, lime juice, pepper and garlic; mix well and set aside. Drain cucumbers; press with hand to remove as much liquid as possible. Pat dry with paper towels. Add to radish mixture and toss until evenly coated. Cover and chill for at least one hour to overnight. Serves 10.

Herb Roasted Potatoes

The combination of rosemary, garlic and thyme makes these potatoes a savory delight!

2 lbs. new redskin potatoes, halved
3 to 4 T. olive oil
coarse salt and pepper to taste
1/4 c. onion, diced
1 T. garlic, minced
1 t. fresh rosemary, minced
1/2 t. fresh thyme, minced
Garnish: fresh rosemary and thyme sprigs

Combine all ingredients except garnish in a large bowl; mix well to coat potatoes. Pour into a 13"x9" baking dish sprayed with non-stick vegetable spray. Bake at 425 degrees for 30 minutes or until potatoes are golden and tender when pierced. Garnish with rosemary and thyme sprigs. Serves 6 to 8.

Brocco-Flower Salad

Combine fresh broccoli with cauliflower for this crunchy treat...pecans add just a hint of sweetness.

1 c. mayonnaise
2 T. red wine vinegar
1/3 c. sugar
1/2 head broccoli flowerets
1/2 head cauliflower flowerets
1/2 c. chopped pecans
1/2 c. red onion, chopped
1/2 c. raisins
8 to 10 slices bacon, crisply cooked and crumbled

Combine mayonnaise, vinegar and sugar; cover and chill. Combine remaining ingredients; add mayonnaise mixture. Mix well and chill before serving. Serves 6.

Mini Carrot Bundt Cakes

As if carrot cake wasn't perfect enough, the sweet mini size of these cakes makes them even tastier!

18-1/4 oz. pkg. carrot cake mix
1/2 c. water
1/2 c. oil
3 eggs, beaten
1/2 c. walnuts, finely chopped
1/2 c. raisins
1/2 c. carrots, grated
8-oz. can crushed pineapple with juice

Combine all ingredients in a large mixing bowl; beat for 2 minutes with an electric mixer on medium speed. Pour into 6 greased mini Bundt® pans. Bake for at 375 degrees for 18 to 20 minutes, or until a toothpick inserted in center comes out clean. Let cool for 10 minutes; turn over onto serving plates. Top with Cream Cheese Drizzle. Makes 6.

Cream Cheese Drizzle:

1/2 c. cream cheese, softened
3 T. butter, melted
2 c. powdered sugar
1/4 c. milk

Combine all ingredients in a bowl; beat with an electric mixer until smooth.

Instead of hiding drinks away in coolers, show them off in a wheelbarrow or a little red wagon. Just fill with ice and stock with frosty beverages!

Old-Fashioned Black Raspberry Buckle

A crumbly topping adds homemade goodness to fresh-picked berries...serve it up warm with a big scoop of ice cream.

1/2 c. water
1-1/2 T. cornstarch
1/2 c. plus 2 T. sugar, divided
1 qt. black raspberries
1 c. all-purpose flour
1-1/2 t. baking powder
1/4 t. salt
1/4 c. butter
1/4 c. milk
1 egg, beaten

Blend water, cornstarch and 1/2 cup sugar; pour over berries in a medium saucepan. Bring to a boil; when mixture thickens, pour into an 8"x8" baking dish and set aside. Sift together flour, one tablespoon sugar, baking powder and salt. Cut in butter until crumbly; set aside. Combine milk and egg; add to flour mixture, stirring just to moisten. Drop by spoonfuls onto hot fruit mixture; sprinkle with remaining sugar. Bake at 400 degrees for 20 minutes or until top is golden. Serves 6.

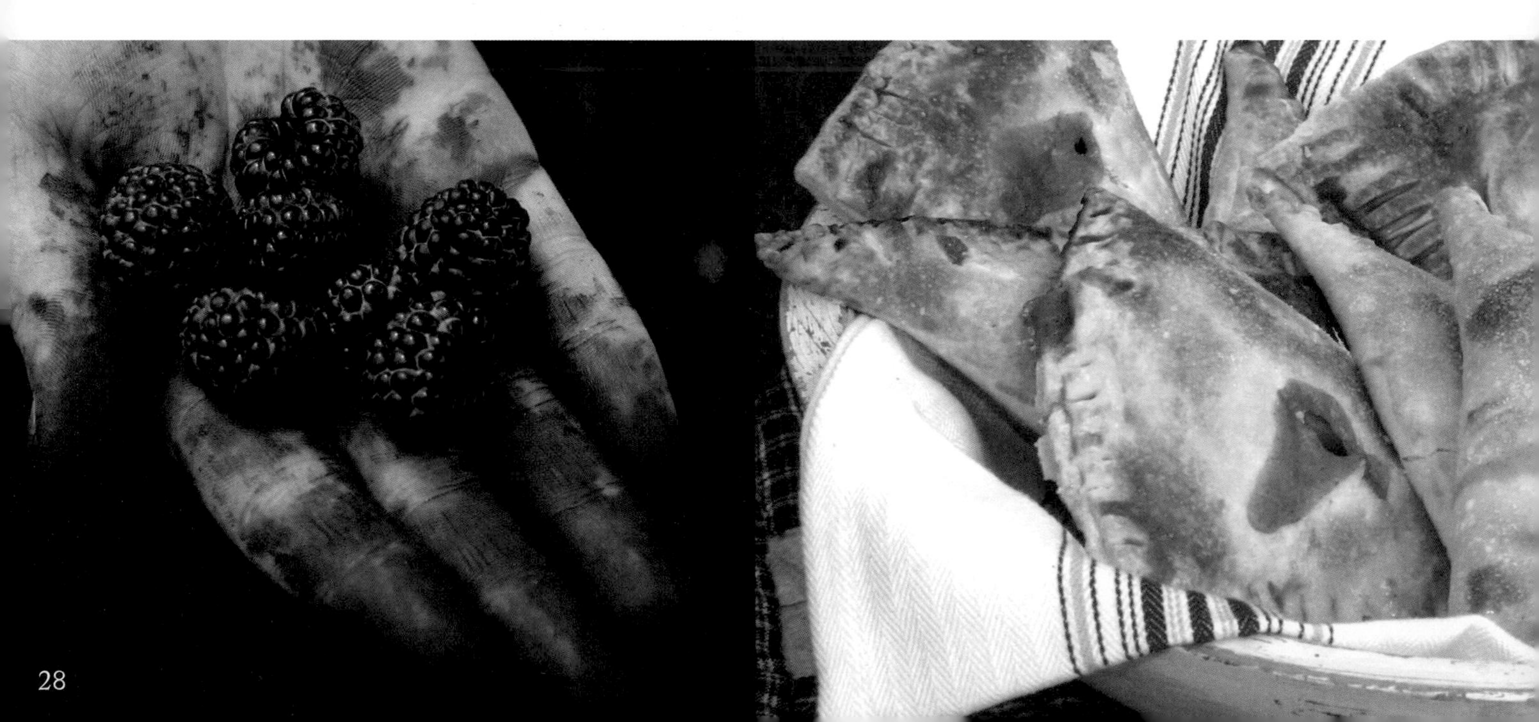

Just Peachy Hand Pies

So easy to make and fun to eat, we like these portable pies for dessert around the picnic table.

1 T. butter
4 t. cornstarch
1/3 c. plus 1 T. sugar, divided
2 lbs. peaches, pitted, peeled and diced
1 t. cinnamon
1/8 t. salt
1 T. lemon juice
4 9-inch pie crusts
1 egg, beaten

Melt butter in a skillet over medium heat. Combine cornstarch with 1/3 cup sugar; add to skillet. Stir in peaches, cinnamon and salt. Cook until mixture thickens and boils, about 25 minutes, stirring frequently. Boil for one minute; remove from heat and stir in lemon juice. Cool completely; set aside. Cut crusts into quarters; spoon 2 tablespoons filling into the center of each quarter, leaving 3/4-inch dough uncovered on each side. Fold dough over filling; press edges together to seal. Transfer pies to 2 ungreased baking sheets. Brush tops of pies with egg; sprinkle with remaining sugar. Cut a one-inch slit in the top of each pie. Bake at 425 degrees for 18 to 20 minutes until golden, rotating baking sheets between upper and lower racks halfway through baking. Remove to wire racks to cool. Makes 16 pies.

Sweet Tea with Lemon

A staple for any summertime get-together, iced tea is sure to quench their thirst...serve it up in old-fashioned Mason jars!

8 c. cold water, divided
1 family-size teabag
1/2 to 3/4 c. sugar
Garnish: lemon slices, fresh mint sprigs

Bring 3 cups water to a boil in a saucepan. Turn off heat; add teabag and let steep 5 minutes. Discard teabag. Pour warm tea over sugar in a large pitcher; stir until sugar is dissolved. Add remaining water and stir until well mixed. Let cool. Serve over ice, garnished with lemon slices and mint. Makes 2 quarts.

Summertime Berry Smoothie

Cool, creamy and full of fruit, this drinkable dessert is fresh and fabulous!

2 c. strawberries, hulled
1 c. mixed berries (blueberries, red and black raspberries)
4-oz. container lemon yogurt
4-oz. container vanilla yogurt
1/2 c. pineapple-flavored orange juice
1 c. ice, crushed
1 T. honey (optional)
Garnish: whipped topping, additional berries, fresh mint sprigs

Combine all ingredients except garnish in a blender; blend until smooth. Pour into 4 glasses; garnish as desired. Serves 4.

Vintage wire carriers are just right for toting iced tea, napkins and flatware to the table. Look for these at flea markets...they come in all shapes and sizes.

A gentle breeze, dappled sunlight and fragrant blossoms. If you're looking for the sunny side of life, you're likely to find it outdoors...on the deck! Combine good friends with delicious food and fresh air, and you'll find everyone lingering long after the sun sets.

Come on over...the menu is mouthwatering and the recipes are a cinch to prepare. Veggie Pizza Triangles and Classic Cobb Salad are sure summertime favorites. Sweet & Sour Shrimp Skewers and Sensational Sirloin Kabobs look like you spent hours in the kitchen, but take just minutes to assemble and grill. Cheese & Garlic Braid is wonderfully simple...our recipe starts with a loaf of frozen bread dough. Can't decide between Chocolate Drenched Strawberries, Key Lime Tarts or Lemon Pound Cake? Try 'em all!

See how easy? Go ahead; throw a party, celebrate and keep the conversation going 'til the stars come out!

dinner on the deck

- CLASSIC COBB SALAD
- MIDSUMMER ITALIAN BREAD SALAD
- VEGGIE PIZZA TRIANGLES
- CHEESE & GARLIC BRAID
- SENSATIONAL SIRLOIN KABOBS
- SWEET & SOUR SHRIMP SKEWERS
- KEY LIME TARTS
- CHOCOLATE-DRENCHED STRAWBERRIES
- LEMON POUND CAKE

Candleholders don't have to be fancy for dinner on the deck...look for inspiration in the kitchen! Mason jars with a twist of wire around the top are easy to hang from nearby branches. Just place a votive inside for a soft glow. Colorful bell peppers and artichokes make simple and elegant holders too. Hollow out the veggies, nestle into a terra cotta pot and add a chunky candle. Voilá!

Classic Cobb Salad

An outdoor favorite, this salad makes an impressive centerpiece on your buffet.

1/4 c. red wine vinegar
3/4 t. salt
1/2 t. dry mustard
1/8 t. pepper
1 clove garlic, crushed
1/2 c. olive oil
1 head lettuce, chopped
1 c. cooked ham, diced
1 c. cooked chicken breast, diced
1/2 lb. bacon, crisply cooked and crumbled
3 eggs, hard-boiled, peeled and quartered
1 tomato, diced
1 avocado, pitted, peeled and diced
1/2 c. crumbled blue cheese
1/2 c. fresh parsley, loosely packed
4 chives, finely chopped

Combine vinegar, salt, mustard and pepper in a jar with a tight-fitting lid; cover and shake. Add garlic and oil to jar; cover and shake well. Set aside. Line a large serving bowl with chopped lettuce; arrange remaining ingredients on lettuce. Shake dressing again; pour over salad or serve on the side. Serves 6 to 8.

Midsummer Italian Bread Salad

This salad has all the fresh taste of bruschetta but in bite-size pieces!

1 loaf Italian bread, cubed
2 cloves garlic, divided
1 c. tomatoes, chopped
1 c. cucumber, chopped
1 c. red onion, chopped
2 c. fresh basil, chopped
2 T. fresh thyme, chopped
1/4 c. olive oil
2 T. balsamic vinegar

Spread bread cubes on a baking sheet; bake at 300 degrees for 5 to 10 minutes, just until dry. Set aside. Peel one clove of garlic; rub garlic around a wooden salad bowl. Combine bread, vegetables and herbs in salad bowl; mince remaining garlic clove and add. Add enough oil and vinegar to coat lightly; toss and serve. Makes 4 to 6 servings.

Veggie Pizza Triangles

Colorful and full of flavor, they're a great way to start the party.

2 8-oz. tubes refrigerated crescent rolls
2 8-oz. pkgs. cream cheese, softened
3 T. mayonnaise
1/2 t. dried basil
1/4 t. garlic powder
1-1/2 c. vegetables, chopped (green and red pepper, carrots, broccoli)
2 T. salad seasoning

Press crescent rolls into a jelly-roll pan, sealing perforations. Bake at 350 degrees for 12 to 15 minutes, until golden. Combine cream cheese, mayonnaise, basil and garlic powder; spread thinly over cooled crust. Top with chopped vegetables. Sprinkle generously with salad seasoning. Cut into triangles. Serve immediately or chill for up to 24 hours. Makes 24 servings.

Cheese & Garlic Braid

Variations on this dish are as easy as choosing your favorite herbs and cheeses... we've listed a few of our favorites!

1-1/2 T. butter
2 cloves garlic, minced
1/2 t. garlic powder
11-oz. tube refrigerated French bread dough
2 T. fresh chives or green onion, chopped
2 T. grated Parmesan cheese

Melt butter over medium heat in a small skillet. Add garlic; sauté 30 seconds or until golden. Remove from heat; stir in garlic powder. Unroll bread dough onto a lightly floured surface; brush with garlic mixture and sprinkle with chives or onion and cheese. Cut dough into 3 strips; roll each strip into a rope shape and braid the strips together. Place on a baking sheet coated with non-stick vegetable spray. Bake at 350 degrees for 17 minutes or until golden. Serve warm. Makes one loaf.

Variations:

For the garlic, chives or green onion and Parmesan, try substituting:

Basil, sun-dried tomatoes and shredded Mozzarella cheese

Rosemary, crispy bacon and crumbled blue cheese

Cinnamon, diced apples and shredded Cheddar cheese

Setting up several locations for food and drinks encourages mingling between guests. Several small tables will do the trick rather than a long buffet...bring out beverage carts used inside to make munchies mobile too!

Sensational Sirloin Kabobs

Red peppers could also be added for an extra punch of color!

1/4 c. soy sauce
3 T. brown sugar, packed
3 T. white vinegar
1/2 t. garlic powder
1/2 t. seasoned salt
1/2 t. garlic pepper seasoning
1/2 c. lemon-lime flavored soda
2 lbs. beef sirloin steak, cut into
 1-1/2 inch cubes
2 green peppers, cubed
2 yellow peppers, cubed
1/2 lb. mushrooms, stems removed
1 pt. cherry tomatoes
3 c. prepared rice

Combine soy sauce, brown sugar, vinegar, garlic powder, seasoned salt, garlic pepper seasoning and soda in a medium bowl; mix well and set aside. Arrange steak in a large plastic zipping bag. Cover with soy sauce mixture, reserving 1/2 cup for basting, and seal. Refrigerate for 8 hours or overnight. Alternately thread steak, peppers, mushrooms and tomatoes onto skewers. Place on a lightly greased grill over high heat; grill for 10 minutes, or to desired doneness. Baste frequently with reserved marinade during the last 5 minutes of cooking. Serve over hot prepared rice. Serves 6 to 8.

Sweet & Sour Shrimp Skewers

Cut wooden skewers in half and make 8 mini kabobs...perfect for munching while mingling.

12 slices bacon, cut in 3-inch pieces and rolled up
12 medium shrimp, peeled
12 whole water chestnuts
1-1/2 c. pineapple, cubed
1/2 c. sweet & sour sauce
2 c. prepared rice

Arrange rolled bacon, shrimp, water chestnuts and pineapple cubes alternately on 4 skewers. Brush with sauce and place on a lightly greased grill over high heat. Grill for about 10 minutes, until bacon begins to brown. Turn and brush with additional sauce several times while grilling. Serve over hot prepared rice. Serves 4.

Key Lime Tarts

Packed with fruity flavor, their mini size makes them irresistible.

22-oz. jar Key lime fruit tart filling
12-ct. pkg. 3-inch tart shells
Garnish: frozen whipped topping, thawed
lime wedges (optional)

Spoon filling into tart shells. Garnish as desired with dollops of whipped topping and lime wedges. Makes one dozen.

Variations:

Spoon raspberry, strawberry or blueberry tart filling into tart shells. Garnish with a dollop of whipped topping and whole berries.

Chocolate-Drenched Strawberries

Simple and oh-so scrumptious, these never fail to please.

1 qt. strawberries
12-oz. pkg. milk chocolate chips
2 T. shortening
white chocolate chips (optional)

Rinse and completely dry strawberries, leaving on stems and leaves; set aside. Combine chocolate chips and shortening in a microwave-safe bowl. Microwave on high setting for one minute; stir. Heat for an additional 45 to 60 seconds, until chocolate is smooth; do not overcook. Dip strawberries in chocolate, leaving top of berry with leaves and stem exposed. Lay dipped berries on a baking sheet lined with wax paper. Place baking sheet in freezer for 2 to 5 minutes, until chocolate hardens. If desired, melt white chocolate and drizzle over berries.

Lemon Pound Cake

This fresh and citrusy treat is made in a fluted tube pan for an extra-special presentation.

1 c. butter, softened
1/4 c. oil
3 c. sugar
5 eggs
3 c. all-purpose flour
1 c. milk
1 t. lemon extract
Garnish: powdered sugar

Beat butter in a large bowl with an electric mixer on medium speed; gradually add oil, beating until well blended. Gradually add sugar, beating well. Add eggs, one at a time, beating well after each addition. Add flour to butter mixture alternately with milk, beginning and ending with flour. Mix just until blended; stir in lemon extract. Pour batter into a greased and floured 10" fluted tube pan. Bake at 300 degrees for 1-1/2 hours or until a toothpick inserted in the center comes out clean. Cool in pan on a wire rack for 15 minutes; remove from pan and place directly on wire rack. Brush Lemon Glaze on sides of cooled cake and spoon over top, a little at a time. Sprinkle with powdered sugar. Serves 10 to 12.

Lemon Glaze:

1/2 c. water
1/4 c. lemon juice
1/2 c. sugar
1 t. lemon zest

Combine ingredients in a small bowl; stir until sugar dissolves.

Dress up napkins in a snap! Tie on bunches of fragrant herbs with ribbon or string jeweled buttons and beads on elastic cord. Vintage or costume jewelry add sparkle too!

Carefree and easy-going, warm-weather days have such a relaxed feel...shoes come off, kids sleep in and the windows stay open. Golden sunshine and a clear blue sky make these days picnic perfect!

Just sneak a peek inside our picnic basket. We're toting along some of our tried & true favorites like Garden-Fresh Potato Salad and Confetti Coleslaw. They're must-haves served with Hot or Cold Fried Chicken and Flaky Buttermilk Biscuits. Herbed Deviled Eggs and Overnight Bread & Butter Pickles make a tangy two-some alongside a Super Stacked Sandwich. And after a few games of Red Rover followed by a sack race or hide & seek, cool 'em off with frosty Razzleberry Lemonade and slices of luscious Blueberry Crumble Bars or Lattice-Topped Cherry Pie.

Picnics are delightful country pleasures to be enjoyed as often as possible. Just choose a shady spot on the grass...ready, set, relax!

pack a picnic

- GARDEN-FRESH POTATO SALAD
- OVERSTUFFED TOMATOES WITH SPICY CORN SALAD
- CONFETTI COLESLAW
- OVERNIGHT BREAD & BUTTER PICKLES
- HERBED DEVILED EGGS
- HOT OR COLD FRIED CHICKEN
- SUPER STACKED SANDWICH
- FLAKY BUTTERMILK BISCUITS
- OATMEAL ICEBOX COOKIES
- BLUEBERRY CRUMBLE BARS
- RAZZLEBERRY LEMONADE
- LATTICE-TOPPED CHERRY PIE

Pack

Garden-Fresh Potato Salad

Fresh green beans and zesty red pepper make this salad anything but ordinary!

1-1/2 lbs. new potatoes, cubed
3/4 lb. green beans, cut into 1-1/2 inch pieces
1 red pepper, chopped
1 red onion, chopped
1/4 c. oil
1/4 c. cider vinegar
2 T. Dijon mustard
1 t. fresh parsley, chopped
1 t. fresh dill, chopped
1 t. sugar
1/2 t. salt

Boil potatoes in water for 10 minutes; add green beans and boil an additional 10 minutes or until potatoes are tender. Drain; allow to cool and transfer to a large serving bowl. Add red pepper and onion; set aside. Whisk together remaining ingredients in a small bowl. Pour over vegetables; toss until well coated. Cover and chill thoroughly before serving. Serves 8 to 10.

Overstuffed Tomatoes with Spicy Corn Salad

Look for tomato varieties in yellow, orange or even striped in the produce section...a small bell pepper will hold the salad in style too!

6 tomatoes
salt to taste
2 c. corn, cooked
1/2 c. shredded Monterey Jack cheese
1/4 c. green pepper, chopped
1/4 c. cucumber, chopped
1/4 c. onion, chopped
1/2 c. buttermilk salad dressing
2 T. fresh parsley, snipped
1/4 t. pepper
1/8 t. cayenne pepper
Garnish: lettuce leaves

Place tomatoes, stem-end down, on a cutting surface. Cut each into 4 to 6 wedges, cutting to, but not through, stem end. Spread wedges apart slightly; sprinkle with salt. Cover; chill and set aside. Combine corn, cheese, green pepper, cucumber and onion in a bowl. Blend dressing, parsley, pepper and cayenne pepper and add to corn mixture; toss gently to coat. Cover and chill. Serve tomatoes filled with corn mixture over lettuce leaves. Serves 6.

Confetti Coleslaw

We like topping a big bowl of this slaw with red and green pepper rings.

6 c. cabbage, shredded
1 c. red cabbage, shredded
1 carrot, peeled and shredded
1/2 red pepper, cut into strips
1/4 c. sweet onion, chopped
3/4 c. mayonnaise-type salad dressing
2 T. lime juice
1 T. fresh dill, snipped
1-1/2 t. sugar
1/4 t. salt
1/4 t. pepper

Combine cabbage, carrot, red pepper and onion in a large bowl; set aside. Blend salad dressing, lime juice, dill, sugar, salt and pepper in a small bowl; mix well. Pour over cabbage mixture; toss to coat. Cover and chill for at least 2 hours; stir before serving. Serves 8 to 10.

Overnight Bread & Butter Pickles

Nothing says "picnic" like the satisfying crunch of a fresh pickle!

7 to 8 pickling cucumbers
1 onion, chopped
1 red pepper, chopped
1 T. kosher salt
2 t. celery seed
1/2 c. honey
1/2 c. white vinegar

If cucumbers have been waxed, peel them. Otherwise, scrub them well and slice thinly. In a large bowl, stir together cucumbers, onion, red pepper, salt and celery seed until well combined. Let stand one hour. Thoroughly mix honey and vinegar. Pour over pickles and stir to blend. Place in a covered glass container and refrigerate. Pickles are ready to eat in 24 hours. Makes 4 cups.

Pack a picnic in a colorful paper tote for each of your guests...just tuck in the silverware, napkins and sandwich plates plus an old-fashioned Mason jar for a cool drink. Clean-up will be a cinch!

Irresistibly sparkly glass bottles of all colors and sizes are spilling from the shelves of our favorite flea markets. We love filling them with easy-to-make herbal vinegars. Look for bottles with rubber seals or lids that screw on tightly. Place a few sprigs of tarragon, rosemary or chives inside and cover with white vinegar. Refrigerate for 2 weeks and enjoy on salads and in marinades!

Herbed Deviled Eggs

Smooth and creamy with the savory taste of Dijon, these eggs can be dressed up easily with our variations below!

6 eggs, hard-boiled, peeled and halved
1/4 to 1/2 c. mayonnaise
1 to 2 t. creamy Dijon mustard
salt and pepper to taste
Garnish: paprika, chopped fresh tarragon, dill or chives, capers

Separate egg yolks and egg whites; set aside whites. Mash yolks in a small bowl; stir in remaining ingredients to desired consistency and taste. Spoon yolk mixture into egg whites; garnish as desired. Makes one dozen.

Variations:

In place of the Dijon mustard, stir in a teaspoon or 2 of creamy prepared horseradish or Thousand Island salad dressing. Try flavored mayonnaises and mustards, too.

Cold
THERM·A·JUG

Hot or Cold Fried Chicken

Delicious when served fresh and hot but for a picnic, there's nothing better than cold fried chicken.

1/2 c. all-purpose flour
1 T. fresh parsley, chopped
1 T. fresh thyme, chopped
1 t. salt
1/2 t. garlic powder
1/4 t. pepper
3 to 3-1/2 lbs. chicken
1 c. buttermilk
1/4 c. oil
1/4 c. butter-flavored shortening

Combine flour, parsley, thyme, salt, garlic powder and pepper in a 9" round shallow dish; set aside. Dip chicken in buttermilk; turn in flour mixture to coat and set aside. Heat oil and shortening in a large skillet; add chicken, skin-side down. Cook over medium-high heat, turning occasionally, until golden and juices run clear, about 35 to 45 minutes. Serves 6.

Super Stacked Sandwich

Use your favorite deli meats and cheese to make a new combination each time!

1/2 c. mayonnaise-type salad dressing
1/4 c. coarse-grain mustard
12-inch round loaf pumpernickel bread, cut in half horizontally
1/2 lb. deli honey ham, thinly sliced
1/2 lb. deli peppered turkey, thinly sliced
1/2 lb. deli chicken breast, thinly sliced
1 tomato, thinly sliced
1 red onion, thinly sliced
8 slices Cheddar cheese
shredded lettuce to taste

Combine salad dressing and mustard; mix well. Spread on inside halves of bread loaf. Layer remaining ingredients on bottom half; top with top half and cut into wedges. Serves 8 to 12.

Variations:

Make a Mexican Super Stacked Sandwich with sliced deli turkey and Pepper Jack cheese on cornmeal-dusted white bread, layered with sliced avocado and topped with salsa. Try an Italian sandwich made with sliced salami and pastrami, provolone cheese, pepperoncini peppers, a splash of Italian salad dressing and a sprinkle of oregano on Italian bread.

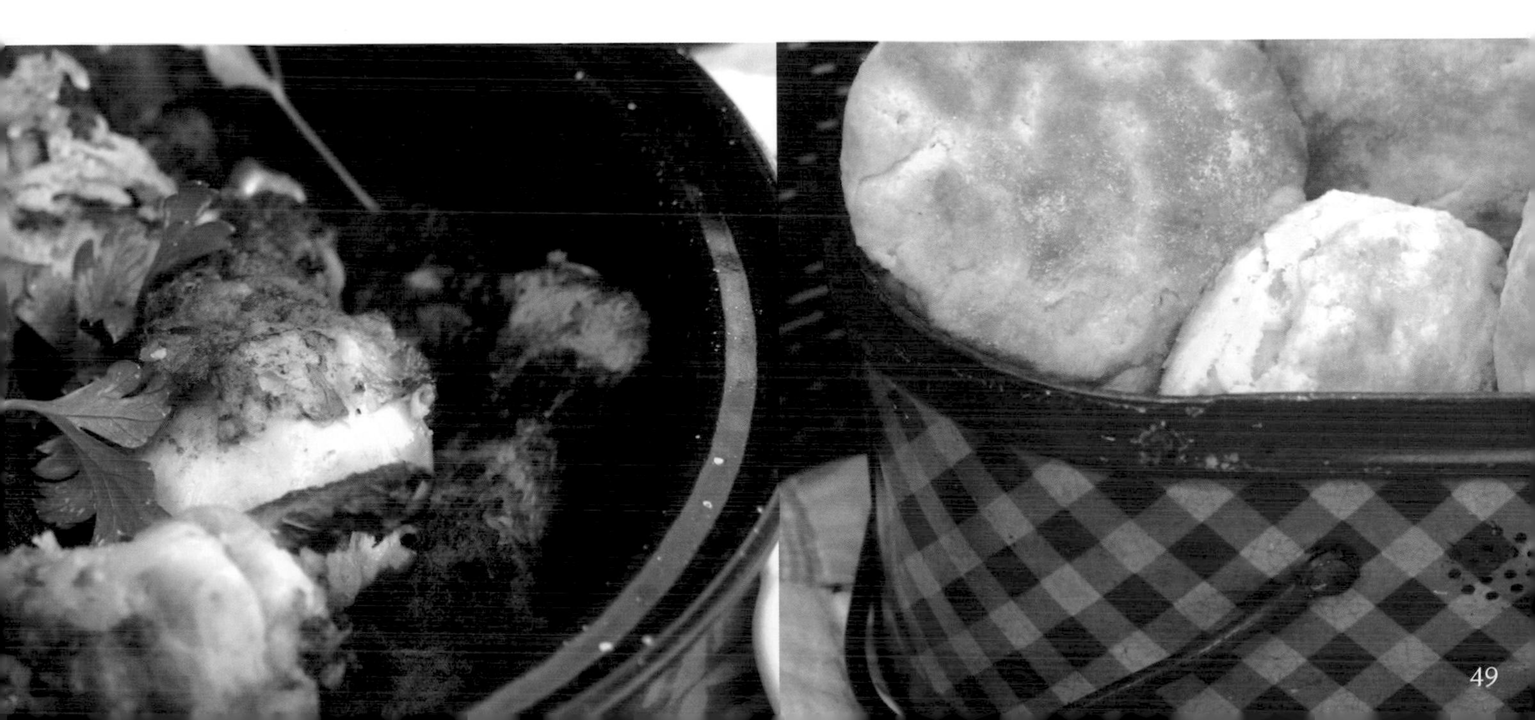

Flaky Buttermilk Biscuits

With a drizzle of honey or a pat of real butter melting in the middle, any way you slice these biscuits, they're heavenly.

2 c. all-purpose flour
2 t. baking powder
1/4 t. salt
2/3 c. butter
1 c. buttermilk

Combine flour, baking powder and salt in a large bowl; cut in butter until coarse and crumbly. Stir in buttermilk just until moistened. Turn dough onto a lightly floured surface; knead until smooth, about 10 times. Roll out dough to 3/4-inch thickness; cut out biscuits with a 2-1/2" biscuit cutter. Place one inch apart on an ungreased baking sheet. Bake at 425 degrees for 12 to 14 minutes or until golden. Makes one dozen.

Oatmeal Icebox Cookies

Slice-and-bake ease with all the sweet homemade taste!

1 c. shortening
1 c. sugar
1 c. brown sugar, packed
2 eggs
1 t. vanilla extract
1-1/2 c. all-purpose flour
1 t. baking soda
1/4 t. salt
1/2 t. cinnamon
3 c. quick-cooking oats, uncooked
1/2 c. chopped pecans

Beat together shortening and sugars with an electric mixer on medium speed until fluffy. Add the eggs and vanilla, beating well. Set aside. Mix flour, baking soda, salt and cinnamon in a separate bowl. Stir flour mixture into shortening mixture, mixing well; stir in oats and nuts. Shape dough into 3 rolls about 2 inches in diameter; wrap in wax paper. Chill for 2 hours up to 3 days. Slice dough 1/4-inch thick; arrange 2 inches apart on ungreased baking sheets. Bake at 350 degrees for 9 to 10 minutes, until golden. Cool on wire racks; store in an airtight container. Makes about 4 dozen.

Blueberry Crumble Bars

This crumbly sweet dessert can be changed on a whim...just change the berries! We like it with blackberries, raspberries or even black raspberries.

1-1/2 c. butter, divided
2/3 c. plus 2 T. powdered sugar, divided
1 t. vanilla extract
3 c. all-purpose flour, divided
3 pts. blueberries
1/2 c. sugar
3 T. cornstarch
2 T. water
1 c. quick-cooking oats, uncooked
1/3 c. brown sugar, packed
1/4 t. cinnamon

Beat one cup butter, 2/3 cup powdered sugar and vanilla with a mixer on medium speed until light and fluffy. Beat in 2-1/2 cups flour on low speed just until combined. Press dough firmly onto bottom of a greased jelly-roll pan. Bake at 375 degrees for 20 minutes or until golden; let cool and set aside. Combine berries, sugar, cornstarch and water in a saucepan. Heat to boiling, stirring frequently; boil for one minute. Remove from heat; set aside. Combine oats, remaining flour, brown sugar and cinnamon in a medium bowl; cut in remaining butter until mixture resembles coarse crumbs. Set aside. Spread berry mixture over cooled crust; sprinkle oat mixture over berries. Bake at 375 degrees for 35 to 40 minutes until berry mixture bubbles and top is golden. Cool completely in pan on wire rack. Sprinkle with remaining powdered sugar. Cut into bars. Makes about 3 dozen.

Since Blueberry Crumble Bars are made in a jelly-roll pan, they're easy to cut creatively for lots of guests. Cut them diagonally into diamonds or use your favorite cookie cutters for an extra-special dessert.

Razzleberry Lemonade

Tart and fruity with just a hint of fizz!

2 12-oz. cans frozen lemonade concentrate, partially thawed
1-1/2 c. frozen red raspberries, divided
2 T. sugar
2-ltr. bottle club soda
1 lemon, sliced

Blend lemonade, one cup raspberries and sugar in a blender; strain to remove seeds. Pour back into blender; add 2 cups ice. Blend until smooth. Divide between two, 2-quart pitchers; add ice to fill. Top with club soda. Garnish individual servings with lemon slices and remaining raspberries. Makes one gallon.

Lattice-Topped Cherry Pie

Want to use fresh sweet cherries instead of tart? Just reduce the amount of sugar by half and add a little lemon juice to taste.

2 c. all-purpose flour
1/8 t. salt
1 c. shortening
1/2 c. cold water
4 c. tart cherries, pitted
1-1/4 c. sugar
2 T. cornstarch
1 T. butter
1/4 t. almond extract
1 egg
1/4 c. milk
1-1/4 t. cinnamon-sugar

Mix flour and salt; cut in shortening with a pastry blender until coarse crumbs form. Stir in water; chill. Roll out half of dough to line a 9" pie plate; set aside. Combine cherries, sugar and cornstarch in a saucepan; let stand for 10 minutes. Bring to a boil over medium heat, stirring constantly. Lower heat; simmer for one minute or until juices thicken. Remove from heat; stir in butter and extract. Pour into crust. Roll remaining dough into a 12-inch circle; cut into 3/4-inch wide strips. Lay strips on pie at one-inch intervals; fold back alternate strips as you weave crosswise strips over and under. Trim crust even with outer rim of pie plate. Dampen edge of crust with water; fold over strips, seal and crimp. Whisk together egg and milk. Brush on crust; sprinkle with cinnamon-sugar. Bake at 375 degrees for 45 to 55 minutes, until golden. Serves 6 to 8.

Barn sales, auctions, flea markets, tag sales...these are our favorite spots for one-of-a-kind finds. Because we know somewhere down a sleepy country lane or just around the next bend, we'll find the best discoveries in the most unlikely places. It's time for a Saturday morning road trip!

Lunch on the road has to be perfectly portable, and our Southwestern Layered Salad and Fruit Trio with Yogurt are just that. Layered and served in pint-sized canning jars, they make lunch fuss-free. Round out this terrific meal with deliciously crunchy Sweet Potato Chips, thirst-quenching Friendship Tea and Chewy Chocolate Chunk Cookies.

Start looking for vintage finds to use in new ways or hidden treasures that spark a sweet memory. And if you're like us, when we find something we love, it's coming home with us...we'll find a spot for it! So, keep the day open and forget your "to-do" list...finding the unexpected is half the fun.

on the road

SOUTHWESTERN LAYERED SALAD

FRUIT TRIO WITH YOGURT

RAINBOW PASTA SALAD

SWEET POTATO CHIPS

OMELET-TO-GO MUFFINS

MEXICALI PEPPE[illegible] MUFFINS

CHEWY CHOCOLATE CHUNK COOKIES

FROM-SCRATCH BROWNIES

LEMON BARS

FRIENDSHIP TEA

Nothing says picnic lunch like stacks and stacks of hearty sandwiches...they're the ultimate lunch on-the-go! Pick up your favorite cheese, sliced deli meats and veggies at the farmers' market. Mix & match them on hearty slices of bread and slice into hand-size halves so they're easy to eat on the run. Wax paper bags make toting them in vintage picnic tins even easier!

Southwestern Layered Salad

Served individually in one-pint Mason jars, this salad is great for taking on the road!

8-oz. container sour cream
3-oz. pkg. cream cheese, softened
10-oz. can tomatoes with green chiles, drained
1 t. cumin
4 c. romaine lettuce, shredded
2 to 3 tomatoes, chopped
15-oz. can black beans, drained and rinsed
15-oz. can corn, drained
1 sweet red onion, chopped
15-oz. can pinto beans, drained and rinsed
2 red peppers, chopped
Garnish: shredded sharp Cheddar cheese, green onion, chopped

Combine sour cream, cream cheese, tomatoes with chiles and cumin in a blender; process until smooth. Chill. Layer vegetables in order given among eight, one-pint Mason jars. Spoon sour cream mixture over top; sprinkle with cheese and green onion. Cover and chill for one hour. Makes 8 servings.

on

Fruit Trio with Yogurt

Enjoyed in the morning before a big day out or as a sweet finish to lunch, this dish couldn't be better.

2 c. blueberries or blackberries
2 c. pineapple tidbits
2 c. strawberries, hulled and sliced
2 c. flavored yogurt

For each serving, layer 2 tablespoons of each fruit in individual 1/2-pint Mason jars. Top fruit with 2 tablespoons yogurt per jar. Makes 8 servings.

Rainbow Pasta Salad

Make it the night before and pack it to go!

12-oz. pkg. rainbow rotini, cooked
1/2 c. red onion, chopped
1/2 c. celery, chopped
1/2 c. carrots, cut in very thin strips
1/2 c. sliced black olives
1/2 red pepper, chopped
1/2 green pepper, chopped
1 c. Cheddar cheese, cubed
1 c. favorite salad dressing

Toss pasta with vegetables and cheese cubes in a large serving dish. Drizzle with salad dressing; chill overnight. Serves 6 to 8.

the road

Sweet Potato Chips

A tasty twist on the lunch time favorite, these can be seasoned any way you like!

1 to 2 sweet potatoes
shortening for deep frying
Garnish: seasoned salt, garlic salt, Creole seasoning or cinnamon-sugar to taste

Peel sweet potatoes and slice very thinly; set aside. In a heavy saucepan, heat 1-1/2 inches of shortening to 365 degrees. Fry potatoes in batches for 3 to 4 minutes, or until golden. Use a slotted spoon to remove; drain on paper towels. Sprinkle to taste with desired seasoning. Makes 4 servings.

Omelet-to-Go Muffins

A whole meal in a muffin, they're so hearty and perfectly portable.

6 eggs
1-1/2 c. cooked ham, finely chopped
1/4 c. shredded Cheddar cheese
1/2 c. fine bread crumbs
3 T. margarine, melted
1 T. fresh chives, finely chopped

Beat eggs until foamy; set aside. Combine remaining ingredients; stir into eggs. Pour into greased muffin cups. Bake at 375 degrees for 20 to 25 minutes, until golden. Serve warm. Makes 12 servings.

Looking for the best finds? Be the earliest bird and get the first look at all the goodies. If you're looking for the best bargains, however, stop back later when the crowds have dwindled a little. Sellers don't want to pack up items if they can sell them that day...start making deals!

Mexicali Pepper Muffins

With the zesty kick of peppers, these spicy snacks are sure to tide you over until lunchtime!

1 c. yellow cornmeal
1 c. all-purpose flour
2 T. sugar
1 T. baking powder
1/2 t. salt
1/2 t. chili powder
1/2 t. dried basil
1/4 c. green pepper, finely chopped
1/4 c. yellow pepper, finely chopped
1/4 c. red pepper, finely chopped
1/4 c. corn
1/4 c. margarine
1 c. milk
2 eggs

Stir together cornmeal, flour, sugar, baking powder, salt and seasonings in a large bowl; set aside. Sauté peppers and corn in margarine in a skillet for 3 to 4 minutes. Beat together milk and eggs; stir together pepper mixture and milk mixture with flour mixture. Pour into greased muffin cups. Bake at 400 degrees for 15 to 20 minutes, until golden. Makes 12 servings.

Tips for Flea Market Shopping

What to Bring

Tape measure and room measurements or better yet, a floorplan so you'll know your bargain will fit once you get it home!

Paint chips or fabric swatches you're trying to match.

A notebook with room to jot down measurements and dealer information...don't forget a pen!

A tote bag roomy enough to hold small finds or a wheeled cart to hold the heavier items.

Bungee cords to secure items for the ride home and bubble wrap for breakables.

A cell phone to touch base with friends aisles away and a digital camera to take snapshots of items to revisit before leaving for the day.

In a backpack: bottled water, snacks, hand wipes and cash!

What to Wear

Dress in layers suitable for chilly mornings and afternoons that heat up. Make sure to wear clothes that you don't mind getting a little dusty.

Comfy shoes that you can walk around and around in...it's sure to be a full day!

Sunglasses or a widebrimmed hat are must-haves, especially for summertime sales.

Chewy Chocolate Chunk Cookies

A chunky twist on everyone's favorite cookie...they travel well too!

1/2 c. butter, softened
1/2 c. brown sugar, packed
1/2 c. sugar
1 egg
1/2 t. vanilla extract
1 c. plus 2 T. all-purpose flour
1/2 t. salt
1/2 t. baking soda
1/2 c. chopped nuts
1/2 c. semi-sweet chocolate chunks

Blend together butter and sugars until creamy. Beat in egg and vanilla; set aside. Combine flour, salt and baking soda; mix well and stir into butter mixture. Fold in nuts and chocolate chunks. Drop by teaspoonfuls, 2 inches apart, on greased baking sheets. Bake at 375 degrees for 10 minutes, or until golden. Makes 2 dozen.

From-Scratch Brownies

No one will say no to these decadent treats after a busy day of browsing!

1 c. butter
6 T. baking cocoa
1 c. sugar
2 eggs
1 c. all-purpose flour
1/2 t. baking powder
1/4 t. salt
1/4 t. vanilla extract

Melt butter with cocoa in a saucepan over low heat. Pour into a mixing bowl; add sugar gradually. Blend in eggs one at a time. Combine flour, baking powder and salt; stir into chocolate mixture. Stir in vanilla. Spread in a lightly greased 8"x8" baking pan. Bake at 350 degrees for 20 to 25 minutes, or until brownies test done in the center. Makes 9 large brownies.

Lemon Bars

Light and fruity, these bars are classic.

2 c. all-purpose flour, divided
1/2 c. powdered sugar
1/4 t. salt
3/4 c. butter, softened
4 eggs
1-1/2 c. sugar
1/2 c. lemon juice
Garnish: powdered sugar

For crust, combine 1-1/2 cups flour, powdered sugar and salt in a medium bowl. Cut in butter with a fork until mixture resembles coarse crumbs. Press into a greased 9"x9" baking pan in an even layer. Bake at 350 degrees for 15 to 18 minutes, until just golden at edges. To make filling, whisk together eggs and sugar in a medium bowl until smooth. Stir in lemon juice, then remaining flour. Pour filling over baked crust. Reduce heat to 325 degrees; bake 25 to 30 minutes, until filling has just set. Let cool for 30 minutes. Cut into 2-inch squares; sprinkle with powdered sugar. Makes 16.

Friendship Tea

On those chilly mornings, nothing's better than warming your hands around a mug of tea with the girls.

1 c. lemonade drink mix
1 c. orange drink mix
1/2 c. instant tea mix
1 t. cinnamon
1/2 t. ground cloves

Combine all ingredients; mix well and store in an airtight container. To serve, put 2 to 3 teaspoons of mix in a mug. Stir in one cup boiling water; adjust to taste. Makes 40 servings.

Remember, dealers add a percentage to their price in anticipation of bargain hunters like you! Be sure to ask for their best price before deciding whether or not to buy. Also, keep in mind that they could offer an even better price if you're picking up multiple items from their booth.

Sandy, breezy, sunny...

warm-weather days seem to cast a drowsy spell that mean it's time for a weekend at the lake. With the kids on summer vacation and a blue sky beckoning, our thoughts turn to summertime fun! We keep it comfortable and carefree...and of course, there's lots of fresh seafood.

The menu is deliciously simple enjoyed right on the beach. Fresh Clam Fritters and Island Fruit Salsa are a terrific twosome, while Salmon BLT's are a new twist on an all-time favorite. And you might have a hard time deciding which shrimp to enjoy...Coconut, Tequila or Zesty BBQ; so you might as well make them all! And for just the right dessert, try Peach-Blueberry Crumble or Double Berry Trifle.

And as the sun begins to dip below the horizon, light the lanterns and unwind...it's been a perfect day.

at the lake

CAPRESE TOMATO SALAD

ORIENTAL SLAW WITH ALMONDS

FRESH CLAM FRITTERS

ISLAND FRUIT SALSA

MANHATTAN CLAM CHOWDER

COCONUT SHRIMP

TEQUILA SHRIMP

SALMON BLT'S

CLAMBAKE IN YOUR KITCHEN

ZESTY BBQ SHRIMP

TOASTED COCONUT CUPCAKES

PEACH-BLUEBERRY CRUMBLE

DOUBLE BERRY TRIFLE

Caprese Tomato Salad

We like to use a combination of red, yellow and orange tomatoes for a burst of color.

3 tomatoes, sliced
1/2 lb. fresh mozzarella cheese, sliced
1 T. fresh basil, chopped
4 T. olive oil
2 T. balsamic vinegar
pepper to taste

Arrange tomato slices in an overlapping circular pattern around a flat serving dish. Arrange cheese slices in between tomato slices. Sprinkle with basil; drizzle with oil and vinegar. Use a fork to lift tomato and cheese slices to allow dressing to cover completely. Add pepper to taste. Let stand for 15 to 30 minutes, to allow flavors to blend. Serves 3 to 4.

Oriental Slaw with Almonds

Full of flavor and pleasantly crunchy, it's a hit at any gathering.

16-oz. pkg. coleslaw mix
3 3-oz. pkgs. ramen noodles, broken
4 green onions, sliced
1 c. sliced almonds
1/2 c. sunflower kernels
1/2 c. oil
6 T. white vinegar
1/4 c. sugar
1 t. salt
1 t. pepper

Toss together coleslaw mix, broken noodles, onions, almonds and sunflower kernels in a large bowl. Set aside. To make dressing, blend together remaining ingredients in a small bowl. Add dressing to salad bowl just before serving; toss well. Makes 8 to 10 servings.

Fresh Clam Fritters

Just like the ones you buy at little stands along the coast, these homemade fritters are surprisingly easy to make.

1 c. all-purpose flour
1 t. baking powder
1 t. salt
1 t. pepper
1/2 t. cayenne pepper
2 ears sweet corn, kernels cut off
1 red pepper, diced
1 yellow pepper, diced
6-1/2 oz. can chopped clams, drained
6 egg whites
2 qts. oil for deep frying

Combine flour, baking powder and seasonings in a large bowl. Stir in corn and peppers; fold in clams and set aside. Whisk egg whites in a small bowl until stiff peaks form. Fold into batter; set aside. Heat oil to 360 degrees in a 4-quart Dutch oven. Drop batter into hot oil by tablespoonfuls; fry a few at a time for one to 2 to 3 minutes or until golden. Drain on paper towels. Makes 3 dozen.

Island Fruit Salsa

Fresh fruit & veggies mingle happily in this dippable delight!

1 c. pineapple, peeled and diced
1 c. mango, peeled and diced
2/3 c. kiwi fruit, peeled and diced
1/2 c. yellow pepper, diced
1/2 c. red pepper, diced
1/2 c. red onion, finely chopped
1/4 c. fresh cilantro, chopped
1 t. lime juice
salt and pepper to taste

Combine all ingredients in a medium bowl. Chill for one hour to allow flavors to blend. Makes about 4-1/2 cups.

Copper wire can be twirled around the base of stemmed glasses...add tiny seashells or beach glass made smooth by the waves to add a touch of the seaside to the table.

Manhattan Clam Chowder

Full of chunky veggies, this version is more brothy than its New England cousin.

2 6-1/2 oz. cans chopped clams
16-oz. can diced tomatoes
2 potatoes, peeled and diced
1 c. onion, chopped
1/2 c. carrots, finely chopped
1 t. salt
pepper to taste
1/2 t. dried thyme

Drain liquid from clams into a large measuring cup; set aside clams. Add enough water to clam liquid to equal 3 cups. Pour into a large saucepan; add remaining ingredients except clams. Cover and simmer for 30 to 35 minutes. Remove from heat; mash vegetables slightly to thicken broth. Add clams; heat through. Serves 6.

Make an ice bowl...it's easier than you think! Place a small, lightweight bowl inside a larger one and criss-cross tape over the top rims so that both are held even. Tuck herbs or delicate oyster, mussel or clam shells in the space between bowls and gently fill with water. Freeze overnight or until solid. Remove bowls and place ice bowl on a charger for the table. Fill with peeled shrimp for a real treat!

MUSSELS

Coconut Shrimp

An interesting mix of sweet and savory, try these on skewers for a portable treat.

1 egg
3/4 c. all-purpose flour, divided
2/3 c. beer
1-1/2 t. baking powder
2 c. flaked coconut
24 medium shrimp, peeled
3 c. oil for deep frying

Combine egg, 1/2 cup flour, beer and baking powder in a medium bowl; set aside. Place remaining flour and coconut in 2 small bowls. Holding shrimp by the tail, dredge in flour, dip into egg mixture and roll in coconut. Arrange shrimp on a wax paper-lined baking sheet; chill for 30 minutes. Heat oil to 350 degrees in a deep fryer. Fry shrimp a few at a time for 2 to 3 minutes, turning once, until golden. Drain on paper towels. Serves 4.

Tequila Shrimp

Makes a mouthwatering meal with a Mexican twist!

2 T. butter
4 cloves garlic, chopped
36 medium shrimp, peeled
1/2 c. tequila
1/2 c. fresh cilantro, chopped
salt and pepper to taste

Melt butter over medium heat in a large skillet; sauté garlic until golden. Add shrimp and cook for 3 minutes. Add remaining ingredients; cook for an additional 2 minutes. Serves 6.

the lake

Salmon BLT's

Anything but ordinary, this sandwich is fresh and delicious.

8 slices thick-cut bacon
1/2 t. sugar
4 6-oz. salmon fillets
salt and pepper to taste
1 lemon, quartered
4 multi-grain buns
8 leaves curly endive
1 to 2 tomatoes, sliced
1 c. alfalfa sprouts
1 red onion, sliced (optional)
Garnish: chipotle mayonnaise

Cook bacon in a skillet over medium heat for 2 minutes. Sprinkle with sugar; cook until crisp. Drain on paper towels. Sprinkle salmon on both sides with salt and pepper. Sauté in drippings in skillet over medium-high heat for about 3 minutes per side, until salmon flakes easily with a fork. Squeeze lemon juice over salmon. Spread bread with Chipotle Mayonnaise. On 4 bun halves, arrange 2 leaves endive, 2 slices bacon, one salmon fillet, 2 tomato slices and 1/4 cup alfalfa sprouts. Top with remaining bun halves. Serves 4.

Chipotle Mayonnaise:

1/2 c. mayonnaise
1/2 t. canned chipotle pepper, minced
1 t. adobo sauce from canned chipotle

Combine all ingredients and mix well. Makes 1/2 cup.

Gather some galvanized buckets and fill about half full with sand. They're perfect for holding lots of taper candles while you dine al fresco. Candlelight without worry of drips or tipping over!

Clambake In Your Kitchen

Everything's piled up in one pot and smells scrumptious simmering on the stove. Serve with your favorite crusty bread.

1 c. yellow onion, chopped
1/4 c. olive oil
1-1/2 lbs. new redskin potatoes
1 T. salt
1/2 T. pepper
1-1/2 lbs. Polish sausage, thickly sliced
2 dozen littleneck clams, scrubbed
1 lb. steamer clams, scrubbed
2 lbs. mussels, cleaned
1-1/2 lbs. large shrimp
2 1-1/2 lb. lobsters
2 c. dry white wine or chicken broth
3 to 4 ears sweet corn, husked and halved

Sauté onion in oil in a heavy 16-quart stockpot until golden. Add remaining ingredients to pot in order given; cover tightly. Simmer over medium-high heat for 15 minutes, just until steam begins to escape; add corn. Lower heat to medium; simmer an additional 15 minutes. Lobsters should be cooked, potatoes and corn tender and shellfish open. Use a slotted spoon to arrange everything on a large platter; top with lobsters cut into serving-size pieces. Season hot broth to taste. Serves 6 to 8.

Zesty BBQ Shrimp

A few dashes of hot pepper sauce really shake up this version of grilled shrimp.

1 c. cider vinegar
2 T. brown sugar
1 T. red pepper flakes
1 t. hot pepper sauce
1/2 c. catsup
1 t. onion powder
salt and pepper to taste
24 to 36 medium shrimp

Combine all ingredients except shrimp in a one-pint glass jar. Shake well; refrigerate sauce for at least 24 hours. Thread shrimp onto metal or wood skewers. Grill for 2 to 3 minutes on each side, brushing generously with sauce. Serves 4 to 6.

Toasted Coconut Cupcakes

Just a little sprinkle of freshly toasted coconut takes these cupcakes from sweet to sensational!

18-1/2 oz. pkg. white cake mix
16-oz. can vanilla frosting
2 c. flaked coconut
2 T. sugar

Prepare and bake cupcakes as cake mix package directs. Let cool; frost. Toss coconut and sugar together; sprinkle on a baking sheet. Toast under broiler for several seconds until golden. Sprinkle over frosting. Makes one dozen.

BAIT & TACKLE
WORM Special
SOFT CRAWS SHRIMP
LAKE SHINERS

Peach-Blueberry Crumble

Serve in your favorite sundae cups with a scoop of vanilla ice cream on top!

4 c. peaches, pitted, peeled and sliced
1 c. blueberries
3/4 c. sugar, divided
2 T. cornstarch
1/2 c. brown sugar, packed
1 c. quick-cooking oats, uncooked
1/4 t. cinnamon
1/4 t. nutmeg
1 egg, beaten
4 T. butter, sliced

Gently toss together fruit, 1/2 cup sugar and cornstarch in a 2-quart baking dish; set aside. Combine remaining ingredients. Stir with a fork until crumbly; sprinkle over fruit mixture. Bake at 375 degrees for 20 to 35 minutes, until topping is golden. Serves 6 to 8.

Double Berry Trifle

With pretty layers and ease of preparation, the trifle is a great way to show off summer's best berries.

1 pound cake, cubed
3-3/4 c. vanilla pudding
12-oz. container frozen whipped topping, thawed
2 c. strawberries, sliced
1 c. blueberries

In a glass bowl, layer half of cake, pudding, whipped topping, strawberries, blueberries; repeat. Chill. Serves 6.

Anything goes when dressing up your outdoor tables! Bold sheets in mixed patterns make festive tablecloths. Just knot those long corners and tuck under. Bring out mismatched chairs from inside and be spontaneous!

Rally together... it's time for a tailgate picnic!

Rally together... it's time for a tailgate picnic! You can hear the low rumble of cheering from the stadium and big brassy sounds of the marching band. So there's no better time to serve up a scrumptious lunch right from the tailgate. And if you need more room, set up a portable table and toss on a checked blanket.

Keep the plans effortless with a make-ahead menu that's a snap to prepare and travels with ease. Pulled Pork BBQ Sandwiches served with Goalpost Apple Slaw and Black Bean-Corn Salsa will keep everyone in high spirits. And be sure to pack lots of bandannas (they make perfect lap-size napkins) when serving sticky-sweet Honey-Glazed Wings. Top off a great meal with chocolatey Classic Texas Sheet Cake or Peanut Butter Swirl Brownies, and everyone will be ready to sing the fight song and cheer on your hometown team!

So whether it's a high school homecoming or a big bowl game, you just can't lose with family, friends, food & fun!

let's tailgate

GOALPOST APPLE SLAW

7-LAYER TACO DIP

BACON-CHEESE DIP

BLACK BEAN-CORN SALSA

CHAMPIONSHIP ARTICHOKE DIP

CHEESY MEXICAN CORNBREAD

HONEY-GLAZED WINGS

PULLED PORK BBQ SANDWICHES

WARM 'EM UP CHILI

GO TEAM MEATBALLS

CLASSIC TEXAS SHEET CAKE

PEANUT BUTTER SWIRL BROWNIES

Let's

Goalpost Apple Slaw

Use your favorite variety of apples...we like Red Delicious and Granny Smith.

2-1/4 c. red apples, cored and thinly sliced
2-1/4 c. green apples, cored and thinly sliced
1 c. sour cream
3 T. lemon juice
1 to 2 T. vinegar
1 T. sugar
3/4 t. salt
1/8 t. pepper
1 T. poppy seed

Lightly toss ingredients in a large bowl until well mixed. Chill for at least one hour. Serves 6 to 8.

7-Layer Taco Dip

Layer upon layer of spicy goodness...add chopped green chiles for an extra kick!

10-1/2 oz. can bean dip
2 avocados, pitted, peeled and mashed
2 t. lemon juice
salt and pepper to taste
1 c. sour cream
1/2 c. mayonnaise
1-1/2 oz. pkg. taco seasoning mix
2 c. tomatoes, chopped
1 c. green onion, chopped
3.8-oz. can sliced black olives, drained
8-oz. pkg. shredded sharp Cheddar cheese
corn or tortilla chips

Spread bean dip in the bottom of a 13"x9" glass serving dish. Mix mashed avocados with lemon juice, salt and pepper; spread over bean dip layer. Blend together sour cream, mayonnaise and taco seasoning; spread over avocado layer. Layer with tomatoes, onion, olives and shredded cheese; chill. Serve with corn or tortilla chips. Makes 10 to 12 servings.

tailgate

Bacon-Cheese Dip

Beware: This dip is highly addictive!

1 lb. bacon, crisply cooked and crumbled
2 8-oz. pkgs. finely shredded Cheddar cheese
2 c. mayonnaise
1 c. chopped pecans
1/2 c. onion, finely chopped (optional)
assorted crackers

Mix together all ingredients except crackers; chill. Serve with crackers. Makes 6 to 7 cups.

Black Bean-Corn Salsa

This salsa adds a dash of spice to your tailgate get-together.

2 15-1/2 oz. cans black beans, drained and rinsed
2 14-1/2 oz. cans diced tomatoes, drained
15-1/4 oz. can corn, drained
1 red onion, diced
1 bunch fresh cilantro, chopped
1 jalapeño, thinly sliced
juice of 1 lime
1/8 t. coarse salt
2 T. tequila (optional)
corn or tortilla chips

Combine all ingredients except chips in a large bowl. Chill overnight; serve with corn or tortilla chips. Makes about 10 cups.

Give the gang plenty of dippers to choose from...hearty crackers, pretzel rods and veggies are all tasty. Make some easy oversized croutons from thick-sliced bread. Just cut into squares, butter and broil until crispy!

Keep a keen eye out for woolly stadium blankets at local flea markets and tag sales. Not only are they great for keeping you and friends toasty during the game, they'll fit right in as clever tablecloths at your next tailgate party.

Championship Artichoke Dip

Try this dip on veggies, toasted bread or pita chips...whatever the dipper, it's sure to disappear in a flash.

2 c. grated Parmesan cheese
2 c. shredded Mozzarella cheese
1 c. mayonnaise
2 cloves garlic, minced
16-oz. can artichoke hearts, drained and finely chopped
1/4 c. green onion, chopped
assorted crackers

Combine all ingredients except onion and crackers in an 8"x8" baking dish; mix thoroughly. Bake at 375 degrees for 45 minutes. Sprinkle with green onion; serve with crackers. Makes 7 cups.

Cheesy Mexican Cornbread

If you'd like a milder version, substitute chopped green chiles for the jalapeños... half the heat with the same great taste.

8-1/2 oz. pkg. corn muffin mix
1 egg, beaten
1/4 c. sour cream
1/3 c. buttermilk
2 to 4 T. diced jalapeños
1/2 c. shredded Cheddar cheese

Combine all ingredients in a mixing bowl; mix well. Pour into a greased 8"x8" baking pan. Bake at 375 degrees for 15 to 20 minutes, until a toothpick inserted in center tests clean. Do not overbake. Cut into squares. Serves 9.

Honey-Glazed Wings

Try this easy sauce on boneless, skinless chicken breasts for a tasty main dish.

2 lbs. chicken wings
pepper to taste
1 c. honey
1/2 c. soy sauce
2 T. oil
2 T. catsup
1 clove garlic, crushed

Sprinkle wings generously with pepper; arrange in a 13"x9" baking dish and set aside. Combine remaining ingredients; mix well and pour over wings. Bake at 350 degrees for 45 minutes, until chicken juices run clear and sauce has thickened. Makes 1-1/2 to 2 dozen.

Pulled Pork BBQ Sandwiches

Keep some of our dry rub mix on hand for roasted or grilled dishes...it adds plenty of flavor to any recipe.

3 to 5 lb. boneless pork roast
1 to 2 T. olive oil
barbecue sauce to taste
8 to 12 sandwich buns

Rub surface of pork with Dry Rub Mix to taste, reserving the rest for another use. Heat oil over medium heat in a large skillet; brown pork on all sides. Place pork in a roasting pan. Bake at 325 degrees until very tender, 3 to 3-1/2 hours. When done, use 2 forks to shred meat. Add barbecue sauce to taste and serve on buns. Makes 8 to 12 sandwiches.

Dry Rub Mix:

1/2 c. paprika
1/4 c. salt
1/4 c. pepper
1/4 c. brown sugar, packed
1/4 c. chili powder
1/4 c. cumin
1 T. cayenne pepper
1 t. onion powder
1 t. garlic powder

Combine all ingredients in a mixing bowl; blend well. Makes 1-3/4 cups.

Warm 'Em Up Chili

A handy seasoning mix makes sure this zesty soup is just right every time.

1-1/2 lbs. ground beef
1 onion, chopped
2 16-oz. cans kidney beans, drained
16-oz. can black beans, drained
16-oz. can pinto beans, drained
15-oz. can corn, drained
14-1/2 oz. can diced tomatoes
14-1/2 oz. can stewed tomatoes
3.8-oz. can black olives, drained
and diced
30-oz. can tomato juice
1-1/2 oz. pkg. taco seasoning mix
salt and pepper to taste

Sauté ground beef and onion in a skillet until browned; drain. Combine all ingredients in a large stockpot. Bring to a boil over medium heat; reduce heat and simmer for 30 minutes. Serves 8 to 10.

Let's

Go Team Meatballs

The whole gang will ask for these savory treats whenever you get together...they make great subs the next day too!

1 lb. ground beef
3/4 c. bread crumbs
1/3 c. onion, finely diced
1 egg, beaten
1 t. salt
1/2 t. celery salt
1/8 t. garlic powder
1/8 t. pepper
5-oz. can tomato sauce
1 c. water
1 T. Worcestershire sauce

Combine first 8 ingredients in a large bowl. Mix well and shape into 1-1/2 inch balls; arrange in an ungreased 13"x9" baking dish. Mix remaining ingredients; pour over meatballs. Cover with aluminum foil; bake at 400 degrees for 45 minutes. Uncover and bake for an additional 15 minutes. Makes 2 to 2-1/2 dozen.

Classic Texas Sheet Cake

Sour cream is the secret to the incredibly moist texture of this family favorite.

1 c. margarine
4 T. baking cocoa
1 c. water
2 c. all-purpose flour
2 c. sugar
1 t. baking soda
1/2 t. salt
1/2 c. sour cream
2 eggs, beaten

Combine margarine, cocoa and water in a saucepan; bring to a boil. Set aside. Sift together dry ingredients; stir in chocolate mixture, then sour cream and eggs. Pour into a greased jelly-roll pan. Bake at 375 degrees for 14 to 18 minutes, until a toothpick tests clean. Top with Chocolate Frosting while still hot. Serves 24.

Chocolate Frosting:

1/2 c. margarine
4 T. baking cocoa
6 T. milk
16-oz. pkg. powdered sugar
1 t. vanilla extract

Combine margarine, cocoa and milk and bring to a boil. Remove from heat and stir in remaining ingredients. Beat well.

Cutting this fudgy cake into one-inch squares makes it portable and extra special too. Serve the chocolatey little bites in mini muffin papers...look for ones in your team's colors for a fun and festive touch!

Peanut Butter Swirl Brownies

Peanut butter and chocolate are always an unbeatable team!

1-1/4 c. all-purpose flour
3/4 t. baking powder
1/2 t. salt
1/2 c. butter
4 1-oz. sqs. unsweetened baking chocolate
4 1-oz. sqs. semi-sweet baking chocolate
1-1/2 c. sugar
2 t. vanilla extract
4 eggs, beaten

Combine first 3 ingredients; set aside. Melt butter and chocolate in a heavy saucepan over low heat, stirring frequently. Remove from heat; stir in remaining ingredients. Stir in flour mixture until well mixed. Spread 2 cups of chocolate mixture in a greased 13"x9" baking pan; top with half of Peanut Butter Swirl in 6 large spoonfuls. Spoon remaining chocolate mixture over and between peanut butter mixture in 6 large spoonfuls. With a knife tip, swirl through both mixtures. Bake at 350 degrees for 30 to 35 minutes, until a toothpick inserted 2 inches from edge comes out nearly clean. Cool in pan on wire rack. Makes 2 dozen.

Peanut Butter Swirl:

1 c. creamy peanut butter
1/3 c. sugar
4 T. butter, softened
2 T. all-purpose flour
1 t. vanilla extract
1 egg

Beat together with an electric mixer on medium speed.

No time before the game to make homemade cut-out cookies? Stop by your local bakery instead... they'll be just as tasty and ready to tote to the tailgate!

Russet reds and vibrant golds...the trees are a blaze of color and the sky is as blue as a robin's egg. The air is crisp and off in the distance is just the faintest hint of wood smoke from the season's first fire in the fireplace...autumn is definitely our favorite time of year!

It's also a great time for harvest gatherings, so invite family & friends to a pumpkin carving party followed by a fall supper. Bowls of Creamy Pumpkin Bisque are a great start to supper, followed by a main course of Pork Loin Roast with Apples, Savory Cornbread Dressing and Sweet Potato-Apple Bake. And don't forget dessert...slices of warm Apple-Pear Crumb Pie with mugs of spicy Hot Mulled Cider make a sweet ending.

When pumpkins dot the farm fields, it's time to slow down and enjoy spending time with those you love most. These near-perfect days are meant for holding on to.

autumn harvest

CRANBERRY WALDORF SALAD

CREAMY PUMPKIN BISQUE

NUTTY BROWN SUGAR SQUASH

SAVORY CORNBREAD DRESSING

GRUYÈRE POTATO GRATIN

SWEET POTATO-APPLE BAKE

GREEN BEANS AMANDINE

PORK LOIN ROAST WITH APPLES

HOMEMADE CLOVERLEAF ROLLS

PUMPKIN-APPLE BUTTER

DRESSED-UP CARAMEL APPLES

CANDY CORN POPCORN BALLS

APPLE-PEAR CRUMB PIE

PUMPKIN ROLL WITH CREAM CHEESE SWIRL

HOT MULLED CIDER

Cranberry Waldorf Salad

A traditional recipe with the added tartness of dried cranberries...try it with almonds too!

1 c. Granny Smith apples, chopped
1 c. Red Delicious apples, chopped
juice of 1-1/2 lemons
1/4 c. celery, chopped
1/4 c. chopped walnuts
1/2 c. sweetened, dried cranberries
1/4 c. grapes, halved
1/2 c. whipping cream, whipped
1/4 c. mayonnaise
1/8 t. nutmeg

Combine apples, lemon juice, celery, walnuts, cranberries and grapes in a large serving bowl; set aside. Combine whipped cream and mayonnaise in a medium bowl; mix well. Toss with apple mixture. Sprinkle with nutmeg; chill before serving. Serves 4.

Baked apples are a special treat for fall and they're so easy to make. Just core 4 Granny Smith, Gala or Golden Delicious apples and set in a baking dish. Mix 1/4 cup each of walnuts, raisins, dried cranberries, softened butter and brown sugar until crumbly. Add mixture to the cores of apples and bake at 350 degrees until tender, about 30 minutes. Simple and scrumptious!

autumn

Creamy Pumpkin Bisque

Serve individual servings in hollowed-out mini pumpkins.

2 T. butter
1 T. green onion, minced
16-oz. can pumpkin
1 c. water
2 T. brown sugar, packed
1/2 t. salt
1/8 t. white pepper
1/8 t. cinnamon
2 cubes chicken bouillon
2 c. half-and-half
Garnish: thinly sliced lemon, fresh minced parsley

Melt butter in a 2-quart saucepan over medium heat; add onion and sauté until tender. Stir in pumpkin, water, brown sugar, salt, pepper, cinnamon and bouillon until mixture begins to boil; cook for 5 minutes. Add half-and-half; heat through, stirring constantly. Ladle into bowls and garnish with lemon and parsley. Serves 3 to 5.

Nutty Brown Sugar Squash

The filling for the squash reminds us of pecan pie!

1-1/2 c. water
1 acorn squash, halved and seeded
2 T. brown sugar, packed and divided
2 t. butter, divided
salt and pepper to taste
1/2 c. chopped pecans, divided

Pour water into a 13"x9" baking dish; add squash cut-side down and bake at 350 degrees for 45 minutes or until tender. Remove from pan; fill each half with one tablespoon brown sugar, one teaspoon butter, salt and pepper to taste and 1/4 cup pecans. Return to oven and bake an additional 10 minutes. Makes 2 to 4 servings.

Savory Cornbread Dressing

A quick cornbread mix cuts prep time for this dressing way down...it'll be ready in a jiffy!

2 8-1/2 oz. pkgs. cornbread mix, prepared and cubed
3/4 c. butter
3/4 c. onion, finely chopped
3/4 c. green pepper, finely chopped
1/2 c. celery, finely chopped
1 T. garlic, minced
2 bay leaves
2 t. salt
1-1/2 t. pepper
1 t. cayenne pepper (optional)
1 t. dried oregano
1/2 t. dried thyme
1/2 t. poultry seasoning
1 c. chicken broth
2 eggs, beaten

Melt butter in a skillet over medium heat. Sauté vegetables, garlic and bay leaves for 2 minutes, stirring occasionally. Stir in seasonings; continue cooking for 5 minutes. Add chicken broth; cook an additional 5 minutes, stirring frequently. Remove from heat; discard bay leaves. Add cornbread and eggs; mix gently. Spoon into a greased 13"x9" baking pan. Bake at 350 degrees until golden, 35 to 40 minutes. Serves 8.

Gruyère Potato Gratin

In this rich & creamy recipe, scalloped potatoes are at their very best.

2 lbs. Yukon Gold potatoes, peeled, sliced and divided
6-oz. pkg. Gruyère cheese, coarsely shredded and divided
salt and pepper to taste
1 c. milk
1 c. whipping cream
nutmeg to taste
Garnish: thinly sliced green onion

Cook potatoes in a saucepan of boiling water for 4 minutes; drain. Arrange one-third of the potatoes in a greased 3-quart casserole dish; sprinkle with 1/2 cup cheese, salt and pepper to taste. Repeat layers once; top with remaining potato slices. Set aside. Combine milk and cream in a heavy saucepan; heat just to boiling. Whisk in nutmeg; pour over potatoes. Sprinkle with remaining cheese. Bake at 400 degrees for 30 minutes, or until golden and potatoes are tender. Garnish with green onion. Makes 4 to 6 servings.

Serve up hearty stews and savory dips in bread bowls instead of dishes. You can find them at the bakery in a variety of sizes...pick up a few small whole wheat rounds for individual servings or a large pumpernickel round to serve the whole gang.

Sweet Potato-Apple Bake

Layers of sweet potatoes and tart apples make the ultimate fall comfort food.

4 sweet potatoes, boiled, peeled and sliced
1/2 c. butter
4 apples, cored, peeled and sliced
1/2 c. sugar
1/2 c. brown sugar, packed
1 to 2 t. cinnamon
1/2 c. water
1/4 c. lemon juice
1/4 c. orange juice

Arrange a layer of sliced sweet potatoes in a greased one-quart baking dish. Dot with butter; sprinkle with sugars and cinnamon. Arrange a layer of apple slices on top; continue layering until all ingredients are used. Combine water and juices; sprinkle over top. Cover and bake at 400 degrees for 45 minutes, or until apples are tender. Makes 4 to 6 servings.

Green Beans Amandine

The fresh flavor of green beans really shines in this dish...the light sauce is more of a dressing.

2 T. butter
3 lbs. green beans, trimmed
3 c. chicken broth
1/2 t. pepper
2 T. cornstarch
1/4 c. water
2 T. lemon juice
1/4 c. slivered almonds, toasted

Melt butter in a large skillet over medium-high heat. Add beans and sauté for 5 minutes. Add broth and pepper; bring to a boil. Reduce heat, cover and simmer for 15 minutes. Dissolve cornstarch in water; add to skillet. Bring to a boil; cook for one minute, stirring constantly. Stir in lemon juice. Sprinkle with almonds. Makes 12 servings.

For a simple table decoration, wrap napkins and silverware with bittersweet vines. If the bittersweet won't bend easily, run under warm water and place in a paper bag to soften. So pretty for a harvest dinner!

Pork Loin Roast with Apples

Tender, baked apples add tart sweetness to this main dish.

3 T. olive oil
5 to 6-lb. boneless pork loin roast, trimmed and tied
salt and pepper to taste
1 c. yellow onion, minced
3 bay leaves
2 T. fresh rosemary, snipped
1 c. balsamic vinegar
1 c. red wine or beef broth
1-1/2 c. pitted dried plums
1 c. dried apricots
4 Granny Smith apples, peeled, cored and quartered

Heat oil in large roasting pan; brown meat on all sides over medium heat. Remove from pan; sprinkle with salt and pepper and set aside. Pour off all but 2 tablespoons drippings; reduce heat. Add onion to pan; cook about 5 minutes or until tender. Add all other ingredients except apples. Bring to a boil; cook for one minute. Remove from heat; return meat to pan. Cover; place in 325-degree oven for 2-3/4 hours. Add apples; cover and bake an additional 15 minutes or until apples are tender. Remove meat and fruit from pan; cover loosely with aluminum foil and set aside. Discard bay leaves; place pan on stovetop over medium-high heat and cook, uncovered, for 15 minutes until liquid is reduced to 1-1/4 cups, stirring and scraping bottom to release drippings. Remove from heat and set aside. Slice pork and arrange on a serving platter with fruit. Spoon a little sauce over roast; serve remaining sauce on the side. Makes 8 to 10 servings.

Homemade Cloverleaf Rolls

Brush with melted butter just before serving for a mouthwatering presentation.

18 frozen bread dough rolls, thawed but still cold
2 T. butter, melted

Spray 12 muffin cups with non-stick vegetable spray; set aside. Use a knife or scissors to cut rolls in half. Arrange 3 halves in each muffin cup. Cover with plastic wrap that has been sprayed with non-stick vegetable spray; let rise until double in size. Remove wrap. Bake at 350 degrees for 15 to 20 minutes, or until golden. Brush tops of hot rolls with melted butter. Makes one dozen.

Pumpkin-Apple Butter

Spread on homemade rolls, quick bread or toast in the morning...any time it's served, it's delicious!

15-oz. can pumpkin
1 c. applesauce
3/4 c. apple juice
1/2 c. brown sugar, packed
1 t. pumpkin pie spice

Combine all ingredients in a saucepan. Bring to a boil over medium heat. Reduce heat; simmer for 1-1/2 hours. Chill; keep refrigerated. Makes 2 pints.

autumn

Dressed-Up Caramel Apples

Instead of popsicle sticks, why not pick a few sturdy twigs to hold these treats?

6 apples
6 wooden popsicle sticks
14-oz. pkg. caramels, unwrapped
2 T. water
Garnish: chopped nuts, multicolored sprinkles, mini candy-coated chocolates

Wash and dry apples; insert sticks into stem end of apples and set aside. Combine caramels and water in a saucepan. Cook and stir over medium-low heat until caramels are completely melted. Dip apples into melted caramel until well coated; let excess drip off. Dip bottoms of apples into desired garnish. Set apples on a plate that has been covered with wax paper, then buttered. Chill for at least one hour. Makes 6.

Candy Corn Popcorn Balls

Chewy and sweet, just like the ones you remember!

8 c. popped popcorn
1 c. candy corn
1/4 c. butter
1/4 t. salt
10-oz. pkg. marshmallows

Combine popcorn and candy corn in a large bowl; set aside. Melt butter in a large saucepan over medium heat; stir in salt and marshmallows. Reduce heat to low and cook, stirring frequently, for 7 minutes or until marshmallows melt and mixture is smooth. Pour over popcorn mixture, stirring to coat. Lightly coat hands with vegetable spray and shape popcorn mixture into 4-inch balls. Makes about 10.

harvest

Apple-Pear Crumb Pie

The crumbly topping on this treat adds something special to this harvest favorite.

9-inch deep-dish pie crust
4 c. Granny Smith apples, peeled, cored and sliced
4 c. pears, peeled, cored and sliced
1/2 c. sugar
1-1/2 T. lemon juice
1-1/2 t. cinnamon, divided
1/8 t. nutmeg
3 T. plus 3/4 c. all-purpose flour, divided
1/2 c. brown sugar, packed
1/4 t. salt
5 T. unsalted butter, cut into 1/4-inch pieces

Freeze pie crust in a 9" deep-dish pie pan for 30 minutes. Combine apples, pears, sugar, lemon juice, one teaspoon cinnamon and nutmeg in a mixing bowl. Add 3 tablespoons flour; toss to coat. Pour into frozen pie crust; bake at 400 degrees for 35 minutes. Combine remaining flour, brown sugar, remaining cinnamon and salt in a food processor; pulse to mix. Add butter; pulse repeatedly until mixture resembles fine crumbs. Pour into a mixing bowl and mix until large, buttery crumbs form. Chill mixture. Remove pie from oven; place on a baking sheet covered with aluminum foil. Top with butter mixture; press lightly to flatten. Reduce oven to 375 degrees; bake an additional 30 to 35 minutes. Cover with aluminum foil during last 15 minutes if necessary. Transfer to wire rack to cool slightly before serving. Serves 8 to 10.

Gather the prettiest autumn leaves you can find and scatter over the tabletop before serving dinner. A hollowed-out pumpkin holding a pot of colorful mums makes an easy centerpiece!

Pumpkin Roll with Cream Cheese Swirl

This cake roll makes such a pretty presentation after the feast.

3 eggs
1 c. sugar
2/3 c. pumpkin
1 t. lemon juice
3/4 c. all-purpose flour
1 t. baking powder
1 T. pumpkin pie spice
1/2 t. salt
1/2 c. chopped nuts

Beat eggs with an electric mixer on high speed for 5 minutes. Add remaining ingredients except nuts; mix well. Spread in a greased jelly-roll pan; sprinkle with nuts. Bake at 375 degrees for 15 minutes. Turn cake out onto a damp tea towel sprinkled with powdered sugar. Roll up cake in towel; let cool on a wire rack for 20 minutes. Unroll cake; immediately spread with Cream Cheese Filling and roll up on long side without towel. Chill for at least one hour; slice. Makes 8 servings.

Cream Cheese Filling:

1 c. powdered sugar
8-oz. pkg. cream cheese, softened
4 T. butter, softened
1/2 t. vanilla extract

Blend all ingredients well.

Hot Mulled Cider

Float a few apple slices and some cinnamon sticks in this warming drink.

2 qts. apple cider
1 orange, quartered
1/4 c. brown sugar, packed
1/4 t. pumpkin pie spice
2 cinnamon sticks
6 whole cloves

Combine all ingredients in a slow cooker; cover and cook on low setting for 2 to 4 hours. Remove orange sections and spices before serving. Makes 10 to 12 servings.

Mulled cider adds the spicy scents of fall...warm up your guests when you serve cider in old-fashioned Mason jars! Wire drink carriers can tote them from kitchen to table and it's sure to really set the mood for your harvest get-together.

Country life...

celebrating the everyday is what country living is all about. And whether it's a cozy cabin or a welcoming inn, a weekend in the country is the perfect place for making memories. Just open the door...the warm setting invites you to linger and enjoy a crackling fire, comfort food and a soft spot to relax.

And if you can't head to the country for a weekend, you can create the warmth of a get-away right in your own home. Toast your tootsies by an early-morning fire with a mug of creamy Hot Cocoa Supreme and Caramel French Toast. And even if sleepyheads are snuggled between layers of flannel blankets, the aromas of Sticky Pecan Buns and Chocolate Chip Pancakes will have them scurrying downstairs in no time.

Serve up some family favorites and make memories to share...it's the comforts of home that mean the most.

weekend in the country

- HOMEMADE WAFFLES WITH BLUEBERRY SAUCE
- SUNRISE SAUSAGE BALLS
- OATMEAL FRUIT SALAD
- CHEESY HASHBROWN POTATOES
- OLD-FASHIONED SPICED APPLES
- JAM-SWIRLED COFFEE CAKE
- FRESH-PICKED FRITTATA
- LEMON-RASPBERRY MUFFINS
- CARAMEL FRENCH TOAST
- STICKY PECAN BUNS
- BROWN-SUGARED BACON
- HOT COCOA SUPREME
- CHOCOLATE CHIP PANCAKES

Spend a weekend away from the hustle & bustle of the city and enjoy the company of loved ones in the quiet countryside. Fill the time together with old-fashioned games, leisurely walks enjoying the weather and plenty of time spent snuggling around a cozy fire. Take along a good book and relax!

Homemade Waffles with Blueberry Sauce

Nothing inspires morning smiles like the unmistakable scent of waffles for breakfast.

2 c. all-purpose flour
1 T. baking powder
1 T. sugar
1/2 t. salt
3 eggs, separated
1-1/2 c. milk
5 T. shortening, melted

Stir together flour, baking powder, sugar and salt; set aside. Beat together egg yolks, milk and shortening; blend into flour mixture until smooth. Stiffly beat egg whites; fold into batter. Pour 1/2 cup batter onto preheated waffle iron; bake as manufacturer directs. Drizzle with Blueberry Sauce. Serves 6.

Blueberry Sauce:

1/2 c. sugar
1 T. cornstarch
1/2 c. water
2 c. blueberries
1 T. butter

Combine sugar and cornstarch in a saucepan; stir in water. Bring to a boil over medium heat; boil for 3 minutes, stirring constantly. Add berries. Reduce heat and simmer for 8 to 10 minutes, until berries burst. Stir in butter until melted. Serve warm.

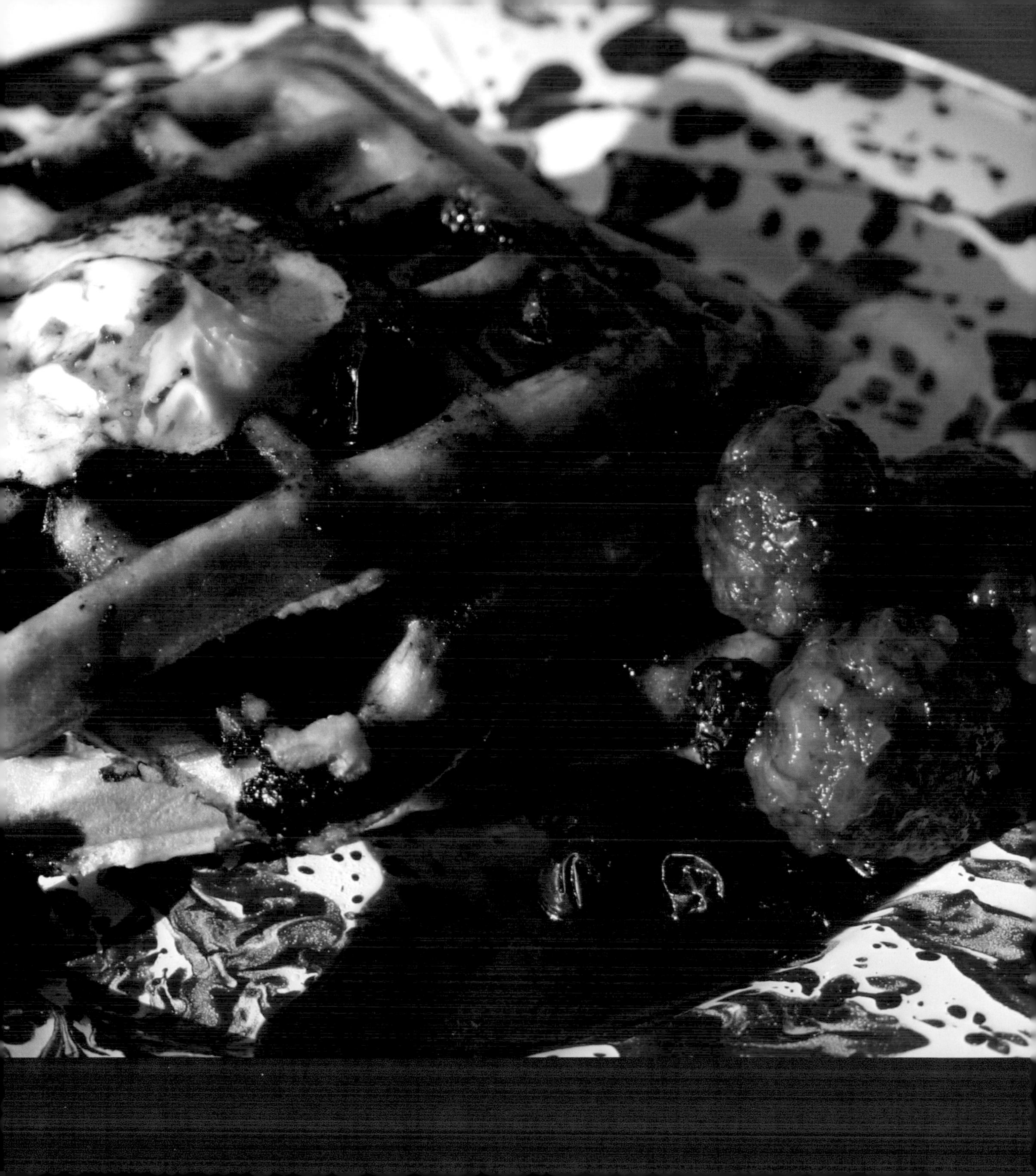

Sunrise Sausage Balls

Serve these immediately or keep them warm in the slow cooker set on low.

1 lb. ground sausage
1/2 c. biscuit baking mix
1/2 c. shredded Cheddar cheese
12-oz. jar apricot preserves

In a large bowl, combine sausage, biscuit mix and cheese. Mix well and form into walnut-size balls. Arrange on ungreased baking sheets. Bake at 350 degrees for 20 to 30 minutes, turning once, until golden. Heat apricot preserves until syrupy; pour over meatballs and toss to coat. Makes 15.

Oatmeal Fruit Salad

Use whatever fruit you happen to have on hand...as long as the total is 2 cups of fruit, it's up to you!

1/2 c. apples, cored, peeled and sliced
1/2 c. peaches, pitted, peeled and sliced
1/2 c. strawberries, sliced
1/2 c. bananas, peeled and sliced
1 T. lemon juice
2 c. instant oats, uncooked
1 c. fruit-flavored yogurt
3 T. orange juice

Toss together sliced fruit in a bowl. Drizzle with lemon juice; stir in oats and set aside. In a separate bowl, combine yogurt and orange juice. Add to fruit mixture; mix well to coat. Chill. Makes 4 servings.

Cheesy Hashbrown Potatoes

A sprinkle of crumbled bacon on top is all the garnish you need for this yummy casserole.

26-oz. pkg. frozen hashbrown potatoes
2 c. shredded Colby cheese
1/4 c. onion, minced
1 c. half-and half or milk
1/2 c. beef broth
2 T. butter, melted
1 t. salt
1/4 t. pepper
1/8 t. garlic powder
Garnish: crisply cooked and crumbled bacon

Combine potatoes, cheese and onion in a large bowl; set aside. Mix remaining ingredients except bacon in a separate bowl; stir into potato mixture until well blended. Spoon into a greased 13"x9" baking dish. Bake at 425 degrees for 45 to 60 minutes. Garnish with bacon. Serves 8 to 10.

Old-Fashioned Spiced Apples

Just like Grandma used to make, there's just no better way to enjoy apples.

6 tart apples, cored, peeled and thinly sliced
1/4 c. brown sugar, packed
2 t. cinnamon
1/4 c. butter

Toss apples with brown sugar and cinnamon; set aside. Melt butter in a large skillet over medium heat; add apples. Cover and cook until tender, 15 to 20 minutes, stirring frequently. Serve warm. Makes 6 servings.

With so many varieties of apples to choose from, keep in mind that some are best for baking and some are best for crunching! The tastiest baking varieties include Golden Delicious, Granny Smith and Rome Beauty while the ones you'll want to enjoy fresh are Red Delicious, Cortland and the sweet Pink Lady.

Jam-Swirled Coffee Cake

Use your favorite flavor of fruity preserves in this breakfast treat!

2 c. all-purpose flour
1/2 c. sugar
1 T. baking powder
1/2 t. salt
1/3 c. butter
1 egg, beaten
3/4 c. milk
1/2 c. apricot preserves
1/2 c. strawberry preserves

Combine flour, sugar, baking powder and salt in a medium bowl; mix well. Cut in butter with a fork or pastry blender until crumbly. Add egg and milk; stir just until moistened. Spread in a well-greased 9"x9" baking pan. Spoon apricot and strawberry preserves over top; use a knife to swirl preserves through batter. Sprinkle evenly with topping. Bake at 400 degrees for 25 to 35 minutes. Use toothpick to check for doneness. Serve warm. Makes 9 to 12 servings.

Topping:

2/3 c. brown sugar, packed
2 T. all-purpose flour
2 T. butter
1/2 c. chopped walnuts

In a small bowl, mix ingredients with a fork until crumbly.

Fresh-Picked Frittata

These are easy to personalize...just let everyone pick their veggies and bake in oven-safe custard dishes until center is set!

1 c. redskin potatoes, diced
1/2 c. onion, diced
2 T. olive oil
1 c. sliced mushrooms
1 c. broccoli flowerets
1/2 c. red pepper, chopped
1/3 c. water
1-1/2 c. shredded Cheddar cheese, divided
8 eggs, beaten
1/2 c. mayonnaise
1/2 t. dried oregano
1/2 t. dried basil
1 T. Italian salad dressing mix

Combine potatoes, onion and oil in a skillet over medium heat; sauté until golden. Add mushrooms, broccoli, pepper and water; cover and cook just until potatoes are tender. Uncover and cook until liquid evaporates. Spoon vegetables into a lightly greased 9-1/2" round deep-dish baking pan; top with half the cheese. Whisk together remaining ingredients except cheese; pour evenly over top. Sprinkle with remaining cheese. Bake at 375 degrees for 40 minutes, or until a knife tip inserted in the center comes out clean. Let stand 5 minutes. Makes 6 servings.

Lemon-Raspberry Muffins

Serve a whole basket full of these moist and tender muffins...delicious!

2 eggs, beaten
1/2 c. milk
1/2 c. lemon yogurt
4 T. butter, melted
1 t. vanilla extract
2 c. all-purpose flour
1 T. baking powder
2/3 c. sugar
2 t. lemon zest, divided
1 t. salt
2 c. raspberries
2 T. lemon juice
1/2 c. powdered sugar

Combine eggs, milk, yogurt, butter and vanilla in a medium bowl; set aside. In a separate bowl, stir together flour, baking powder, sugar, one teaspoon zest and salt. Stir egg mixture into flour mixture; fold in berries. Spoon into greased muffin cups. Bake at 350 degrees for 18 to 20 minutes, until tops spring back when touched. Combine lemon juice, powdered sugar and remaining zest; brush over warm muffins. Makes one dozen.

Caramel French Toast

Prepare this the night before...when you get up in the morning, just pop it in the oven!

1 c. brown sugar, packed
1/2 c. butter
2 T. corn syrup
12 slices bread
6 eggs, beaten
1-1/2 c. milk
1 t. vanilla extract
1/4 t. salt

Combine sugar, butter and syrup in a small saucepan. Cook over medium heat until thickened, stirring constantly. Pour into a 13"x9" baking dish. Arrange 6 slices bread in dish; top with remaining slices. Blend remaining ingredients; pour evenly over bread. Cover and chill for 8 hours. Uncover and bake at 350 degrees for 40 to 45 minutes, or until golden. Serve immediately. Makes 6 servings.

Sticky Pecan Buns

Oooey, gooey goodness...guaranteed smiles at the breakfast table!

3/4 c. chopped pecans
24 rolls frozen bread dough
4-oz. pkg. butterscotch cook & serve pudding mix
1/2 c. butter
3/4 c. brown sugar, packed
1 t. cinnamon

Sprinkle pecans in a greased 13"x9" baking pan; arrange rolls over pecans. Sprinkle pudding mix over rolls; set aside. Melt butter in a small saucepan over low heat; stir in brown sugar and cinnamon until sugar melts. Pour butter mixture over rolls. Cover pan with aluminum foil sprayed with non-stick vegetable spray. Let rolls rise for 8 hours or overnight. Bake at 350 degrees for 30 minutes. Invert pan onto a baking sheet or large tray and serve warm. Makes 2 dozen.

Brown-Sugared Bacon

This morning treat is the perfect mixture of salty and sweet.

1/2 c. brown sugar, packed
1 t. cinnamon
8 slices thick-sliced bacon, halved

Combine sugar and cinnamon in a small bowl. Dip each piece of bacon into mixture to coat. Twist each piece and arrange on an aluminum foil-lined broiler pan. Bake at 350 degrees for 15 to 20 minutes, until bacon is crisp and sugar is bubbly. Place bacon on aluminum foil to cool. Makes 16 pieces.

Before taking off for the weekend, put together a basket full of goodies to take along. Include some yummy coffee or tea you've been saving for a special occasion plus graham crackers, chocolate and marshmallows for making s'mores. Throw in some special treats to pamper yourself too...bubble bath, scented lotion or bath salts!

Hot Cocoa Supreme

Topped with marshmallows and chocolate chips or even sprinkled with crushed mints, it's a terrific way to warm up.

3/4 c. sugar
1/2 c. baking cocoa
1/4 t. salt
5 c. water
2 c. milk
1 c. whipping cream
1 t. vanilla extract

Combine sugar, cocoa and salt in a saucepan; whisk in water. Bring to a boil over high heat, stirring until sugar is completely dissolved. Reduce heat to medium; add milk and cream. Heat through without boiling; keep warm over low heat. Serves 6 to 8.

Chocolate Chip Pancakes

No need for syrup but be sure to have plenty of napkins on hand!

1 c. milk
2 eggs, beaten
2 c. buttermilk biscuit baking mix
1/4 t. cinnamon
1/2 c. mini semi-sweet chocolate chips
Garnish: frozen whipped topping, thawed and mini semi-sweet chocolate chips

Combine milk, eggs, biscuit mix and cinnamon, stirring until moistened. Fold in chocolate chips, being sure not to over-blend. Drop by 1/4 cupfuls onto a hot, greased griddle; flip over when bubbles appear around edges. Cook each side until lightly golden. Top with a dollop of whipped topping and chocolate chips, if desired. Makes 12 to 16 pancakes.

Comfort food... oh, how it soothes!

Nothing else nourishes us like a home-cooked meal. Comfort food not only warms us head to toe, it warms our hearts as well.

We'd like to share some of our best-loved recipes...ones that remind us of special times spent with family & friends. Nothing compares to Just Like Mom's Meatloaf served alongside Twice-Baked Potato Casserole. Old-Fashioned Chicken Pot Pies have a flaky crust and are filled with tender chicken and vegetables in a rich broth...so good beside Sweet Potato Knots drizzled with butter. Four-Cheese Mac & Cheese is so golden and delicious that kids big and little will be asking for seconds! And nothing ends a meal like Chocolate Bread Pudding or Butter Rum-Glazed Applesauce Cake.

Comfort food is really just good, homestyle cooking that makes us feel warm & cozy inside. It brings back fond memories and when we make it for those we love, we're sharing those good memories all over again.

winter warmers

FRENCH ONION SOUP

WEDGE SALAD WITH ROQUEFORT DRESSING

TWICE-BAKED POTATO CASSEROLE

FOUR-CHEESE MAC & CHEESE

JUST LIKE MOM'S MEATLOAF

OLD-FASHIONED CHICKEN POT PIES

SWEET POTATO KNOTS

CHOCOLATE BREAD PUDDING

BUTTER RUM-GLAZED APPLESAUCE CAKE

French Onion Soup

This hearty and savory soup is always welcome on a chilly winter day.

2 T. butter
4 onions, sliced
3 c. beef broth
1-1/2 c. water
1 T. Worcestershire sauce
1/4 t. pepper
1/8 t. dried thyme
1 T. sherry (optional)
1 c. French bread, cubed and toasted
1/2 c. Gruyère cheese, shredded

Melt butter in a saucepan over low heat. Add onions; cook for 20 minutes, stirring occasionally. Add broth, water, Worcestershire sauce, pepper, thyme and sherry, if using. Increase heat; bring to a boil. Reduce heat, cover and simmer for 5 minutes. Divide into 4 oven-safe soup bowls; top with bread cubes, then cheese. Place under a broiler just until cheese melts. Serves 4.

Wedge Salad with Roquefort Dressing

Crisp and crunchy, this salad makes an impressive presentation and is extra special with dressing made from scratch!

1 head iceberg lettuce
1/2 c. Roquefort cheese, crumbled
1 c. olive oil, divided
1/3 c. white wine vinegar
1/3 c. lemon juice
2 t. sugar
1/4 t. salt
1/4 t. garlic salt
1/4 t. pepper
Garnish: chopped tomatoes, crisply cooked and crumbled bacon

Cut head of lettuce into quarters; set aside. Place cheese in a small bowl; gradually stir in 1/2 cup oil. Pour into a one-pint jar. Add remaining ingredients; cover tightly and shake well. Chill for at least one hour; shake again before serving. Place one wedge of lettuce on each serving plate; drizzle with dressing. Garnish with tomatoes and bacon, if desired. Serves 4.

Twice-Baked Potato Casserole

What could be more comforting than warm and cheesy potatoes?

6 baking potatoes
1/4 c. butter, softened
1 c. shredded Cheddar cheese
1-1/4 t. salt
1/4 t. pepper
1 c. hot milk
3 green onions, finely chopped
1/2 c. sour cream
Garnish: shredded Cheddar cheese, chopped green onion

Pierce potatoes' skins with a fork; bake at 425 degrees for one hour. Cut potatoes in half; scoop out into a large bowl and mash. Add butter, cheese, salt and pepper; mix well. Add hot milk; beat until fluffy and cheese is melted. Stir in onion and sour cream; blend. Spoon potato mixture into an 11"x7" baking dish. Sprinkle with additional cheese and onion. Bake for 15 minutes at 375 degrees, until heated through. Makes 8 servings.

Four-Cheese Mac & Cheese

We like rotini because the spirals really grab the cheese...yum!

1/4 c. all-purpose flour
1/8 t. pepper
2-1/2 c. milk
1/2 c. grated Parmesan cheese
1/2 c. shredded sharp Cheddar cheese
6 oz. pasteurized processed cheese spread, cubed
2 oz. cream cheese, cubed
3 c. rotini pasta, cooked
1/3 c. onion-flavored Melba toast, crushed
1 T. butter, melted

Combine flour and pepper in a saucepan; whisk in milk until smooth. Bring to a boil over medium heat; once boiling, cook for one minute stirring constantly. Reduce heat; add cheeses, stirring until melted. Remove from heat; stir in pasta and pour into a 9"x9" baking dish. Combine toast crumbs and butter; sprinkle on top. Bake at 350 degrees for 30 minutes or until bubbly and golden. Serves 6.

Once mashed potatoes are mixed to your liking, add in a little something special! Some of our favorite stir-ins include cooked, crumbled bacon, shredded cheese, horseradish, fresh chives or green onion. Any way they're served, you know they'll love 'em!

Just Like Mom's Meatloaf

Top with buttery mashed potatoes, French fried onions and chopped green onions...simply divine.

2 eggs, beaten
8-oz. can tomato sauce
3/4 c. cracker crumbs
1/4 c. onion, chopped
1/4 c. green pepper, finely chopped
1 T. Worcestershire sauce
1 t. salt
1/2 t. pepper
1-1/2 lbs. ground beef
1/2 c. catsup
2 t. mustard
2 T. brown sugar, packed

Combine first 8 ingredients in a medium bowl; add ground beef and mix well. Shape into a loaf; place in a 9"x5" loaf pan. Bake at 350 degrees for one hour. Combine catsup, mustard and brown sugar; pour over meatloaf and bake an additional 10 to 15 minutes. Serves 6.

Old-Fashioned Chicken Pot Pies

Hearty filling and golden pastry served in individual casseroles...what could be better?

6 T. butter
1/2 c. onion, chopped
1/2 c. all-purpose flour
1 t. salt
1/4 t. white pepper
3 c. chicken broth
3 c. cooked chicken, cubed
10-oz. pkg. frozen peas and carrots, cooked and drained
2 c. potatoes, cooked and cubed
17.3-oz. pkg. frozen puff pastry sheets, thawed

Heat butter in a saucepan over medium heat. Sauté onion until tender and golden. Blend in flour, salt and pepper; add broth and whisk well. Cook until thick and bubbly; add remaining ingredients except puff pastry. Divide evenly among 6 individual casserole dishes; set aside. Cut puff pastry into 6 squares to fit the tops of dishes; cut a steam vent in the center of each with a mini cookie cutter. Place pastry tops on casserole dishes; set dishes on a baking sheet. Bake at 400 degrees until pastry is golden, about 10 to 15 minutes. Serves 6.

Sweet Potato Knots

Tender, flaky and oh-so good...worth the effort!

1 env. active dry yeast
1 c. warm milk
3/4 c. canned sweet potatoes, mashed and liquid reserved
3 T. butter, melted and divided
1-1/4 t. salt
2 egg yolks, beaten
5 c. bread flour, divided
Garnish: melted butter

Dissolve yeast in milk in a large bowl; let stand 5 minutes. Add sweet potatoes, one tablespoon butter, salt and egg yolks; whisk together, adding a tablespoon or 2 of sweet potato liquid if mixture is too stiff. Add 4-1/2 cups flour, stirring until a soft dough forms. Turn out onto a floured surface; knead until smooth and elastic, about 8 minutes. Add remaining flour one tablespoon at a time until dough no longer sticks to hands. Place in a large bowl sprayed with non-stick vegetable spray. Turn to coat; cover. Let rise in a warm place for 45 minutes, until double in bulk. Punch down; let rest for 5 minutes. Divide into 24 portions. Shape each into a 9-inch rope, then into a knot, tucking top end under roll. Arrange rolls on 2 parchment paper-lined baking sheets. Spray lightly with non-stick spray; cover and let rise 30 minutes, until double in bulk. Bake on bottom 2 oven racks at 400 degrees for 8 minutes. Rotate baking sheets and bake an additional 7 minutes, until golden. Cool on wire racks; brush with melted butter. Makes 2 dozen.

Chocolate Bread Pudding

Just like Grandma's with a twist of cocoa to tempt your sweet tooth.

2 c. milk
6 slices bread, cubed
1/2 c. sugar
1/3 c. baking cocoa
2 eggs, separated and divided
2 T. butter, melted
1 t. vanilla extract
1/2 c. chocolate chunks
Garnish: whipped cream,
 baking cocoa

Heat milk in a large saucepan just until tiny bubbles form; remove from heat. Add bread; stir until smooth. Add sugar, cocoa and egg yolks; stir until well blended. Add butter and vanilla; set aside. Beat egg whites until stiff peaks form; fold into mixture along with chocolate chunks. Pour into a lightly greased 8"x8" baking dish; set dish in a larger pan with one inch of hot water in it. Bake at 350 degrees for 40 minutes, or until firm. Garnish with whipped cream and baking cocoa; serve warm or cold. Serves 6.

Butter Rum-Glazed Applesauce Cake

The warm glaze poured over the cake is enough to make anyone want to stay inside and get cozy.

1/3 c. butter
3/4 c. sugar
1 c. applesauce
1 apple, cored, peeled and chopped
1 t. vanilla extract
1-1/4 c. all-purpose flour
1 t. baking soda
1 t. cinnamon
1/2 t. salt

Melt butter in a saucepan over medium heat. Cook and stir for 2 to 2-1/2 minutes, just until butter begins to brown. Immediately remove from heat; stir in sugar, applesauce, apple and vanilla. Set aside. Combine remaining ingredients in a large bowl; stir in applesauce mixture. Pour into a greased 8"x8" baking pan. Bake at 350 degrees for 25 minutes, until a toothpick inserted in center comes out clean. Pour warm Butter Rum Glaze over cake. Let cool 30 minutes; serve warm. Makes 9 servings.

Butter Rum Glaze:

2 T. butter
1 c. powdered sugar
1/2 t. rum extract
3 to 4 t. half-and-half or milk

Melt butter in a saucepan over medium heat. Cook and stir for 2 to 2-1/2 minutes, just until butter begins to brown. Immediately remove from heat; stir in remaining ingredients until spreadable and smooth.

Big fuzzy mittens make cute cozies for silverware at the table. Tie them together with a length of matching yarn or jute and hang over the chairbacks too...they'll even hold placecards!

Christmas cheer...

you can feel the magic in the air. December is here, snowflakes are swirling and frost tinsels the trees, making it the perfect time for a jolly holiday gathering. You've been talking about doing it for years, so make this year the one you host a holiday open house!

Pull out all the stops with an amazing menu that's surprisingly simple to prepare. Seafood Lasagna complements tangy Bruschetta with Cranberry Relish, while Lemon Shrimp and Very Berry Meatballs are anything but ordinary. No one can resist Prosciutto-Wrapped Breadsticks and Antipasto Kabobs...they'll disappear quickly! Top the evening off with Sparkling Ruby Sipper and Fudgy Fondue, and you'll find a sweet ending to a truly unforgettable open house.

So, deck your halls, walls and mantels, then settle in to enjoy the happiest, most magical time of year.

holiday open house

RED & GREEN SALAD

PROSCIUTTO-WRAPPED BREADSTICKS

ANTIPASTO KABOBS

SPINACH SWIRLS

SPARKLING RUBY SIPPER

CHEERY CHEESE TRUFFLES

NUTTY CHICKEN SKEWERS

VERY BERRY MEATBALLS

LEMON SHRIMP

BRUSCHETTA WITH CRANBERRY RELISH

SEAFOOD LASAGNA

CHEDDAR BISCUITS WITH GARLIC BUTTER

FUDGY FONDUE

RED VELVET CAKE

Red & Green Salad

5-oz. pkg. spring mix greens
5-oz. pkg. red leaf lettuce
5-oz. pkg. baby spinach
Garnish: thinly shaved Romano cheese, crumbled feta cheese, thinly sliced red onion, dried cranberries

Toss greens with Raspberry Salad Dressing in a large salad bowl. Divide among 8 salad plates. Arrange garnishes and Spicy Pecans on top. Serves 8.

Raspberry Salad Dressing:

1 T. raspberry vinegar
2 t. lime juice
1 t. sugar
1/2 t. salt
1/4 c. oil
1/2 c. dried cranberries

Combine ingredients in a blender; purée until smooth.

Spicy Pecans:

1/4 c. powdered sugar
1/2 t. salt
1/4 t. allspice
1/8 t. nutmeg
1/8 t. cayenne pepper
1/3 c. pecan halves

Combine sugar, salt and spices in a small bowl. Rinse pecans with water; drain but do not let dry. Add pecans to sugar mixture; toss well to coat. Arrange on a baking sheet sprayed with non-stick vegetable spray. Bake for 10 minutes at 350 degrees, stirring occasionally.

Making a cranberry ice ring couldn't be easier! Just fill a tube pan one inch deep with water and freeze until solid. Add an additional 1/4 inch water and half a bag of whole cranberries over the ice. Return pan to freezer until set. Add an additional inch of water, more cranberries and freeze until solid. To unmold, run briefly under warm water to loosen and set on a plate. Add sprigs of fresh and festive greenery for a lovely centerpiece.

holiday

Prosciutto-Wrapped Breadsticks

If prosciutto is not readily available, you can always substitute thinly sliced ham.

6 slices prosciutto
1/2 c. chive & onion-flavored cream cheese, softened and divided
18 long thin bread sticks
Garnish: dried parsley

Lay prosciutto slices on a cutting board; spread each slice with 2 teaspoons cream cheese. With a long sharp knife, cut each slice lengthwise into thirds. Wrap each strip of prosciutto around a bread stick, starting at one end and wrapping toward middle. Dip wrapped end of each bread stick into remaining cream cheese, then into parsley. Makes 18.

Antipasto Kabobs

Off the tray and onto a skewer, these little beauties are portable!

1/3 c. olive oil
1/3 c. balsamic vinegar
1 T. fresh thyme, minced
1 clove garlic, minced
1 t. sugar
9-oz. pkg. cheese-filled tortellini, cooked
5-oz. pkg. salami, thinly sliced
12-oz. jar artichoke hearts, drained and quartered
5-3/4 oz. jar green olives with pimentos, drained
16-oz. jar banana peppers, drained
1 pt. cherry tomatoes

Combine oil, vinegar, thyme, garlic and sugar; set aside. Alternately thread remaining ingredients in order given onto sixteen, 6-inch skewers. Arrange skewers in a single layer in a glass or plastic container; drizzle with marinade. Cover; refrigerate for 2 to 24 hours, turning occasionally. Drain marinade before serving. Makes 16 servings.

Spinach Swirls

With a creamy filling, these roll-ups are so easy to make ahead of time.

8-oz. pkg. cream cheese, softened
1/2 c. sour cream
1/2 c. mayonnaise
1-oz. pkg. ranch dip mix
2-oz. jar bacon bits
1/4 c. red pepper, diced
4 green onions, chopped
2 10-oz. pkgs. frozen chopped spinach, thawed and drained
10 8-inch flour tortillas

In a medium mixing bowl, combine cream cheese with sour cream and mayonnaise. Stir in dip mix; add bacon bits, red pepper, onions and spinach. Mix well. Spread mixture on tortillas to within 1/2 inch of edge; roll up tightly. Wrap each tortilla in plastic wrap; chill overnight. At serving time, cut each roll into one-inch slices. Makes 6 dozen.

Sparkling Ruby Sipper

Fruity and fizzy, it'll add plenty of punch to the party!

12-oz. can frozen pink lemonade concentrate
20-oz. pkg. frozen strawberries
2 c. water
1 qt. pineapple sherbet
2 c. lemon-lime soda, chilled

In a blender, combine half each of lemonade concentrate, strawberries, water and sherbet. Blend until smooth; pour into a punch bowl. Repeat with remaining ingredients. Refrigerate until serving time. Just before serving, gently pour in soda; stir to mix. Makes 14 servings.

Classic luminarias with a Christmas twist! Place red and white peppermint swirls or red cinnamon candies in Mason jars and nestle a votive candle in the center. They'll add a bright and cheery glow to the walkway, entryway or dining room table.

Cheery Cheese Truffles

Truffles don't have to be sweet treats...these savory bite-size beauties are the proof!

8-oz. pkg. cream cheese, softened
1/2 c. finely shredded Monterey Jack or Muenster cheese
1/8 t. cayenne pepper
2 to 3 oz. Gorgonzola or smoked Gouda cheese
Garnish: dried parsley, paprika, poppy seed, chopped pecans, chopped sweetened, dried cranberries

Blend cream cheese, shredded cheese and cayenne in a small bowl. Cover and chill for one hour. Cut Gorgonzola or Gouda cheese into 30 small cubes. For each truffle, form a scant 2 teaspoonfuls of cream cheese mixture into a ball around a cheese cube. (Return mixture to refrigerator if it becomes too soft to handle.) Roll truffles in desired garnishes; chill until serving time. Makes 2-1/2 dozen.

Nutty Chicken Skewers

Hearty and sweet, these saucy skewers are a quick fix under the broiler.

3 boneless, skinless chicken breasts
1/2 c. creamy peanut butter
1 c. water
1 T. soy sauce
1/4 t. ginger

Place chicken breasts between 2 layers of plastic wrap; pound to 1/4-inch thickness. Cut into 6-inch by 1/2-inch strips; set aside. Whisk together peanut butter and water in a small saucepan until smooth; stir in soy sauce and ginger. Heat over medium-low heat for 3 to 5 minutes, stirring occasionally. Marinate chicken strips in peanut butter mixture for at least 30 minutes. Thread chicken onto wooden skewers that have been soaked in water; broil until golden and juices run clear. Makes 1 to 1-1/2 dozen.

holiday

Very Berry Meatballs

For the party, keep these warm in a slow cooker on its lowest setting.

1 lb. ground beef
1 c. herb-seasoned dry bread crumbs
1 c. whole-berry cranberry sauce, divided
1 egg
1-1/2 t. salt
1/2 t. pepper
1 t. dried basil
1/2 t. dried thyme
2 T. oil
1 c. beef broth
1/2 c. orange juice
1 T. all-purpose flour

Combine ground beef, bread crumbs, 1/2 cup cranberry sauce, egg and seasonings. Mix well; shape into one-inch balls. Cook in hot oil until browned, about 10 minutes; drain. Combine broth and remaining cranberry sauce in a saucepan; heat until gently boiling. Stir together juice and flour in a bowl until smooth; add to mixture in saucepan, stirring until thickened. Reduce heat; add meatballs and simmer for 15 to 20 minutes. Makes about 3 dozen.

Lemon Shrimp

Purchased phyllo shells make these tarts so simple to make.

3/4 c. dill-flavored sour cream dip
1 t. lemon juice
1/2 t. lemon zest
30 frozen mini phyllo dough shells, baked
2 T. capers
30 medium shrimp, cooked and peeled
Garnish: fresh dill sprigs, lemon zest

Stir together dip, lemon juice and zest in a small bowl. Fill each baked shell with about one teaspoon dip mixture; sprinkle with capers. Arrange one shrimp, tail up, in each shell. Garnish as desired with fresh dill and lemon zest. Chill until serving time. Makes 2-1/2 dozen.

Bruschetta with Cranberry Relish

A holiday twist on an Italian favorite, this version combines the sweetness of fruit with the distinctive taste of blue cheese.

1 baguette, cut into 1/4-inch thick slices
1 to 2 T. olive oil
1 t. orange zest
1 t. lemon zest
1/2 c. chopped pecans
1/2 c. crumbled blue cheese

Brush baguette slices lightly with olive oil. Arrange on a broiler pan; toast lightly on one side under broiler. Turn slices over; spread with Cranberry Relish. Sprinkle with combined zests, then with pecans and blue cheese. Place under broiler just until cheese begins to melt. Makes 18 to 20.

Cranberry Relish:

16-oz. can whole-berry cranberry sauce
6-oz. pkg. sweetened, dried cranberries
1/2 c. sugar or more to taste
1 t. rum extract
1 c. chopped pecans

Stir together all ingredients in a medium bowl.

Jingle bells add the sounds of the season to your holiday open house. Look for packages of bells in different sizes at the craft store. String them on raffia or satiny ribbon and hang from doorknobs, on the backs of chairs or add them to your swags of greenery on the mantel or across a doorway. So festive and so easy!

Seafood Lasagna

Cheese lovers on your list? This decadent delight has four cheeses in all!

16-oz. pkg. mushrooms, minced
1-1/2 c. onion, chopped
2 T. fresh thyme, chopped
3 cloves garlic, minced and divided
2 t. olive oil
1/4 c. white wine or chicken broth
2 6-1/2 oz. cans crabmeat, drained
10 to 12 large raw shrimp, peeled and halved lengthwise, shells reserved
2 c. water
1-1/2 t. celery salt
1 t. fennel seed
1-1/4 c. crumbled feta cheese
1 c. cottage cheese
1/4 c. fresh basil, finely chopped
1 T. lemon juice
1/4 c. all-purpose flour
1 c. milk
1/4 c. grated Parmesan cheese
8-oz. pkg. lasagna, cooked
8-oz. pkg. shredded mozzarella cheese
1/4 c. fresh parsley, chopped

Sauté mushrooms, onion, thyme and 2 cloves garlic in oil over medium heat for 10 minutes. Add wine (or chicken broth) and bring to a boil; cook for 1-1/2 minutes, until liquid almost evaporates. Remove from heat; stir in crabmeat and set aside. Combine shrimp shells, water, celery salt and fennel seed in a saucepan. Bring to a boil; cook for 15 minutes, until reduced to 1-1/2 cups liquid. Strain liquid; set aside. Combine feta and cottage cheeses, basil, lemon juice and remaining garlic; set aside. Place flour in a small saucepan; gradually whisk in milk and shrimp stock. Bring to a boil; reduce heat and simmer for 5 minutes, until thickened. Remove from heat; stir in Parmesan. Spray a 13"x9" baking dish with non-stick vegetable spray; spread 1/2 cup sauce in bottom of dish. Layer as follows: 4 strips lasagna, slightly overlapping, 1/3 of cheese mixture, 1/3 of crab mixture, 1/3 of shrimp, 2/3 cup sauce and 2/3 cup mozzarella. Repeat layers twice, ending with mozzarella. Bake at 375 degrees for 40 minutes, until golden. Let stand for 15 minutes; sprinkle with parsley. Makes 8 servings.

Capture the true meaning of the holidays with a different kind of gift-giving. Ask guests to bring a pair of gloves or mittens with them to the open house. Collect them at the door and, after the festivities, donate them to a local shelter or school. That's the spirit!

Cheddar Biscuits with Garlic Butter

An irresistible complement to our Seafood Lasagna, these biscuits are yummy all by themselves too!

2 c. biscuit baking mix
2/3 c. milk
1/2 c. shredded Cheddar cheese
3/8 t. garlic powder, divided
1/4 c. butter, melted

Mix baking mix, milk, cheese and 1/8 teaspoon garlic powder to form a soft dough. Drop by teaspoonfuls on an ungreased baking sheet. Bake for 8 to 10 minutes, until golden. Mix melted butter and remaining garlic powder; brush over biscuits. Makes 10 to 12.

Fudgy Fondue

Fondue is one of our party favorites... mingling is guaranteed with everyone gathered around the goodies.

4 1-oz. sqs. sweet baking chocolate, chopped
4 1-oz. sqs. semi-sweet baking chocolate, chopped
2/3 c. light cream
1/2 c. powdered sugar
1 t. vanilla extract
assorted dippers: cut-up fruit, cubed pound cake, marshmallows

Combine chocolates, cream, sugar and vanilla in a heavy saucepan over low heat. Cook and stir until melted and smooth. Pour into a fondue pot; keep warm over low heat. Serve with fruit, cake or marshmallows for dipping. Makes 6 to 8 servings.

Red Velvet Cake

When you serve the deep red slices of this cake, you're sure to be greeted with plenty of oohs and aahs.

1/2 c. shortening
1-1/2 c. sugar
2 eggs
2-oz. bottle red food coloring
2 t. baking cocoa
1 t. salt
2-1/2 c. all-purpose flour
1 c. buttermilk
1 t. vanilla extract
1 t. baking soda
1 t. vinegar

Blend together shortening, sugar and eggs; set aside. In a separate bowl, mix together food coloring and cocoa; add to shortening mixture. Add salt, flour, buttermilk and vanilla. Alternately add baking soda and vinegar until just blended. Pour into 2 greased, floured 8" round cake pans. Bake at 350 degrees for 30 minutes; cool. Spread with frosting to make a 2-layer cake. Serves 6 to 8.

Frosting:

3 T. all-purpose flour
1 c. milk
1 c. sugar
1 c. shortening
1 t. vanilla extract

Combine flour and milk in a saucepan; cook over medium heat until thick. Cool. Blend together sugar, shortening and vanilla until fluffy; add to flour mixture. Beat until light and fluffy.

Chocolate-dipped peppermint sticks or stirring spoons make tasty take-home gifts for your guests. Put a few in a cello bag, tie with a ribbon and add a tag that thanks them for sharing the holiday festivities with you!

Sugar, spice...

and sprinkles! The excitement of the holiday season begins the day we bring out the flour, sugar and eggs to make Christmas cookies. All of a sudden we're kids again, and one cookie just isn't enough. We all have our tried & true favorites, and it just wouldn't be the holidays without them. So this year, why not share those best-loved treats at a cookie exchange?

We've given you lots of goodies to choose from. Some are classics, like Easiest Ever Sugar Cookies and Peanut Butter Fudge, while others are familiar, but with a new twist. Maybe Peppermint Snowballs and Fudgy Mint Cheesecake Bars will be the new "must-haves" with family & friends. And no one can resist yummy Hint of Mint Biscotti!

Everyone loves swapping treats for the holidays. And when they're made with love and wrapped with imagination, they bring out the kid in all of us.

cookie exchange

- CHECKERBOARD COOKIES
- WHOOPIE PIES
- MINTY CANDY CANE COOKIES
- JAM-FILLED LINZER COOKIES
- HO-HO-HOLIDAY SNACK MIX
- GUMDROP COOKIES
- PEPPERMINT SNOWBALLS
- LEMON ICEBOX COOKIES
- DIPPED GINGERBREAD STARS
- EASIEST EVER SUGAR COOKIES
- SPARKLING SUGAR COOKIES
- EVERYTHING'S IN 'EM COOKIES
- PEANUT BUTTER BUTTONS
- FUDGY MINT CHEESECAKE BARS
- CHRISTMAS CRINKLE COOKIES
- BUCKEYES
- WHITE CHOCOLATE-CRANBERRY BARS
- HINT OF MINT BISCOTTI
- CRISPY ROCKY ROAD BITES
- MINT CREAM WAFERS
- PEANUT BUTTER FUDGE

The cookies are the stars of the table but you can certainly add holiday cheer with some simple decorations too! Try filling an apothecary jar with brightly colored glass ornaments, scatter vintage-style postcards over the table and break out all those old-fashioned tin cookie cutters and pile in your favorite mixing bowl. Nothing says Christmas like cookies, after all!

Checkerboard Cookies

Always a hit at exchanges, they look like you spent all day on them!

1 c. butter, softened
1 c. sugar
1 egg
1 egg yolk
1 t. vanilla extract
2-3/4 c. all-purpose flour
2 T. baking cocoa

Blend together butter and sugar. Beat in egg, egg yolk and vanilla; gradually add the flour. Divide dough into 2 portions; beat cocoa into one portion. Form dough into 2 balls; shape each into 2 ropes. Working with 4 ropes (2 of each color) press a light dough rope and a dark dough rope together. Repeat with remaining ropes. Place one pair of ropes on top of the other, alternating light and dark doughs. Press together to form a long roll; repeat with remaining dough. Wrap each roll in plastic wrap; refrigerate 4 hours, until firm. Slice 1/4-inch thick; arrange one inch apart on parchment paper-lined baking sheets. Bake at 350 degrees for 8 to 10 minutes. Makes 2 dozen cookies.

GLASS

Whoopie Pies

The creamy filling makes these chocolate sandwiches so yummy.

1/2 c. shortening
1 c. sugar
1 t. baking soda
1/8 t. salt
1-1/4 c. buttermilk
1 egg
1 t. vanilla extract
2 c. all-purpose flour
2/3 c. baking cocoa

Beat together shortening, sugar, baking soda and salt with an electric mixer on medium speed. Beat in buttermilk, egg and vanilla; set aside. Stir together flour and cocoa; stir into shortening mixture. Drop by rounded tablespoonfuls 2 inches apart onto ungreased baking sheets. Bake at 350 degrees for 8 to 10 minutes, until edges are firm. Cool on wire racks. Spread 2 tablespoons filling on flat side of half of the cookies; top with remaining cookies, flat-side down. Store, covered, in a cool place or the refrigerator. Makes 14 Whoopie Pies.

Filling:

3/4 c. milk
1/4 c. all-purpose flour
3/4 c. butter, softened
2 c. powdered sugar
1 t. vanilla extract

Combine milk and flour in a small saucepan. Cook and stir until thickened and bubbly; cook and stir for 2 minutes more. Let cool. Beat together butter and sugar with an electric mixer on medium speed until fluffy; add vanilla. Gradually beat in milk mixture; beat on high for one minute, or until smooth and fluffy.

exchange

Minty Candy Cane Cookies

Easy spritz dough is dressed up for the holidays with a dip of white chocolate and a sprinkle of peppermint.

3/4 c. butter, softened
1/2 c. sugar
1 t. baking powder
1 egg
1/2 t. peppermint extract
1-3/4 c. all-purpose flour
6 1-oz. sqs. white baking chocolate
1 T. shortening
1/3 c. peppermint candies, finely crushed

Beat together butter, sugar and baking powder with an electric mixer on medium speed. Add egg and extract; blend well. Beat in as much flour as possible with mixer; stir in any remaining flour. Pack dough into a cookie press fitted with a 1/2" star plate. Force dough through press to form 4-inch long sticks about one inch apart on ungreased baking sheets; bend into candy-cane shape. Bake at 375 degrees for 7 to 9 minutes, or until edges are firm but not brown. Let cool on a wire rack. Melt white chocolate and shortening in a small heavy saucepan over low heat, stirring frequently. Dip the end of each cane into chocolate, letting excess drip off. Place on wax paper; sprinkle with crushed candies. Let harden. Makes 5 dozen cookies.

Make a special centerpiece that's related to all the holiday baking going on. Display mixing bowls lined with towels and overflowing with cookies for munching. Use cake stands, stacked or singly, to display pretty tarts and bars along with old-fashioned ribbon candy...and don't forget the tabletop trees!

Jam-Filled Linzer Cookies

Get creative with these...use any cutter you like and add a tiny star in the center!

2-1/2 c. all-purpose flour
1 c. whole blanched almonds
2/3 c. sugar
1 t. cinnamon
1/4 t. ground cloves
1/4 t. salt
1-1/4 c. butter, sliced
1/4 t. almond extract
1 t. lemon zest
1 c. seedless red or black currant or raspberry jam
Garnish: powdered sugar

Combine flour, nuts, sugar, spices and salt in a food processor; pulse until nuts are finely ground. With machine on, add butter a few slices at a time; process. Add extract and zest; process until dough begins to form moist clumps. Form dough into 2 flat disks on plastic wrap; cover with plastic wrap and chill. Roll out dough 1/4-inch thick on a floured surface, one disk at a time. Cut out with large star-shaped cookie cutters; cut out a small star from the center of half the cookies. Arrange cookies one inch apart on parchment paper-lined baking sheets. Bake at 325 degrees just until light golden around edges, about 20 minutes. Let cool on baking sheets for 2 minutes; remove to wire racks to cool completely. Place jam in a small bowl; stir until smooth. Spread a thin layer of jam on the bottoms of solid stars. Arrange stars

with cutouts on a baking sheet, top-side up; sprinkle with powdered sugar. Sandwich cookie tops with bottoms. Place remaining jam in a frosting cone; pipe jam into cut-outs to fill. Makes 2 dozen.

Ho-Ho-Holiday Snack Mix

Dried cranberries, holiday marshmallows or shaped baking bits will mix merrily with this snack...use your favorites!

10-1/2 oz. pkg. bite-size crispy honey nut corn & rice cereal squares
8-oz. pkg. candy-coated chocolates
8-oz. pkg. holiday candy corn
9-oz. pkg. raisins
12-oz. jar dry-roasted peanuts

Mix all ingredients together; store in an airtight container. Makes 3 pounds.

Gumdrop Cookies

They look like they've been sprinkled with confetti...how fun!

1 c. butter, softened
1/2 c. sugar
1/2 c. brown sugar, packed
2 T. milk
1 t. vanilla extract
2-1/2 c. all-purpose flour
1 t. baking powder
3/4 c. gumdrops, finely chopped

Blend together butter and sugars; beat in milk and vanilla and set aside. Stir together flour and baking powder; blend into butter mixture. Stir in gumdrops. Shape dough into two, 14-inch rolls. Wrap in plastic wrap; chill thoroughly. Cut into 1/4-inch slices; arrange on ungreased baking sheets. Bake at 375 degrees for 10 minutes. Makes about 4 to 5 dozen cookies.

Peppermint Snowballs

Christmas classics with a hint of mint that makes them extra special.

1/2 c. peppermint candies, finely crushed and divided
1/4 c. plus 1/3 c. powdered sugar, divided
1 c. butter, softened
1 t. vanilla extract
2-1/4 c. all-purpose flour
1/4 t. salt

Combine 1/4 cup crushed candies and 1/4 cup powdered sugar; set aside. Beat together butter, remaining powdered sugar, remaining candies and vanilla with an electric mixer on medium speed. Stir in flour and salt. Shape into one-inch balls; arrange one inch apart on ungreased baking sheets. Bake at 325 degrees for 12 to 15 minutes, or until set but not brown. Immediately remove from baking sheets; roll in reserved candy mixture. Let cool completely on a wire rack; roll again in candy mixture. Makes about 2-1/2 dozen cookies.

exchange

Lemon Icebox Cookies

Light and crispy, they're just right with a cup of tea!

3/4 c. sugar, divided
3/4 c. brown sugar, packed
1 c. butter, softened
1-1/2 t. vanilla extract
1 egg
1 egg, separated
3 c. all-purpose flour
1-1/2 t. baking powder
3/4 t. salt
2 T. lemon juice
1 T. lemon zest
3/4 c. finely chopped nuts

Combine 1/2 cup sugar, brown sugar, butter, vanilla, egg and egg yolk; blend well. Add flour, baking powder, salt, lemon juice and zest; mix well. Shape dough into two, 1-1/2 inch thick rolls; wrap in wax paper. Refrigerate for one hour, or until firm. Combine nuts and remaining sugar in a small bowl. Slightly beat egg white. Brush chilled dough with egg white; roll in nut mixture, pressing in nuts firmly. Slice dough 1/4-inch thick. Place slices one inch apart on greased baking sheets. Bake at 400 degrees for 5 to 7 minutes, or until lightly golden. Immediately remove from baking sheets; cool on wire racks. Makes 7 dozen cookies.

A chandelier will provide a cheery welcome overhead when decorated with greenery, vintage cookie cutters and colorful glass berries. After the party, remove the cookie cutters and leave the rest up all winter long!

Be Merry

Dipped Gingerbread Stars

Spicy and sweet with a jacket of white chocolate, they're irresistible.

1 c. shortening
1 c. brown sugar, packed
3/4 c. molasses
3/4 c. buttermilk
2 eggs
4-1/2 c. all-purpose flour
1 T. ground ginger
2 t. baking soda
1 t. salt
Garnish: white chocolate chips, melted

Blend shortening and brown sugar together; add molasses, buttermilk and eggs. Blend well; set aside. In a separate bowl, mix flour, ginger, baking soda and salt; blend into shortening mixture. Mix well; refrigerate overnight. Roll out dough 1/4-inch thick on a lightly floured surface; cut out with a star cookie cutter. Arrange on ungreased baking sheets; bake at 400 degrees for 10 to 12 minutes. Let cool completely; dip half of each cookie into melted white chocolate. Makes about 5 dozen cookies.

Easiest Ever Sugar Cookies

So easy to mix up, even the kids can help!

3.4-oz. pkg. instant vanilla pudding mix
1/2 c. sugar
1/2 c. butter
1 egg
1-1/2 c. all-purpose flour
1 t. baking powder

Blend together pudding mix, sugar and butter; stir in egg and set aside. Mix flour with baking powder; blend thoroughly into pudding mixture. Chill dough until firm. Roll out to 1/8-inch to 1/4-inch thickness on a lightly floured surface; cut with desired cookie cutters. Arrange on lightly greased baking sheets. Bake for 8 to 9 minutes at 350 degrees. Makes 2 to 3 dozen cookies.

Mini cookie cutters make invitations a keepsake too! Use a permanent marker to date each cutter and then tie onto the front of the invitation with a length of raffia or ribbon. On the inside, write all the details for the party...your guests can even use their cutter when making their goodies to exchange.

Sparkling Sugar Cookies

Be sure to have plenty of red cinnamon candies, sprinkles, jimmies and colored sugars on hand to dress these up!

3/4 c. butter, softened
1 c. sugar
1 t. vanilla extract
2 eggs
2-1/2 c. all-purpose flour
1 t. baking powder
1/2 t. salt

Beat butter, sugar, vanilla and eggs in a large bowl with an electric mixer on medium speed. Stir in flour, baking powder and salt, using hands if necessary so mixture holds together. Refrigerate for one hour, or until firm. Roll out half of dough at a time 1/8-inch thick on a lightly floured surface; use cookie cutters to cut into desired shapes. Arrange cookies about 2 inches apart on ungreased baking sheets. Bake at 375 degrees for 6 to 8 minutes, or until lightly golden. Cool on a wire rack. Frost and decorate as desired. Makes about 4 dozen cookies.

Decorator Frosting:

2 c. powdered sugar
2 T. milk
1/2 t. vanilla extract
1/8 t. salt
food coloring, if desired

Mix all ingredients until smooth and spreadable, adding more milk if necessary to achieve desired consistency.

exchange

Everything's In 'Em Cookies

Everything but flour that is...feel free to substitute pecans or walnuts for peanuts!

6 eggs
1 c. margarine, softened
1 lb. brown sugar
2 c. sugar
1/8 c. vanilla extract
6 T. corn syrup
1-1/2 lbs. creamy peanut butter
4 t. baking soda
9 c. quick-cooking oatmeal, uncooked
1/2 lb. semi-sweet chocolate chips
1/2 lb. peanuts
1/2 lb. candy-coated chocolate pieces

Mix ingredients in order listed in a large bowl. Drop by rounded teaspoonfuls onto ungreased baking sheets. Bake at 350 degrees for 12 to 16 minutes. Makes 10 to 12 dozen cookies.

Peanut Butter Buttons

Classic cookies with a kiss of chocolate in the middle...oh-so good.

14-oz. can sweetened condensed milk
3/4 c. creamy peanut butter
2 c. biscuit baking mix
1 t. vanilla extract
1/4 c. sugar
48 milk chocolate drops, unwrapped

Blend condensed milk and peanut butter until smooth. Add baking mix and vanilla; mix well. Shape into one-inch balls; roll in sugar. Arrange 2 inches apart on ungreased baking sheets. Bake at 375 degrees 6 to 8 minutes, until golden; do not overbake. Immediately press a chocolate drop in the center of each cookie. Cool completely on wire racks. Makes about 4 dozen cookies.

Short on time? Dress up ready-made cookies from the bakery with piped-on icing or by dipping them in chocolate! Double-dipped chocolate sandwich cookies or peanut butter sandwich cookies drenched in melted white chocolate... they're both so easy!

Terrific Take-Home Tips

Round flat tins, woven berry baskets, paper take-out boxes in festive holiday prints and glass jars with screw-on lids all make great take-home totes for cookies!

Brown or white paper lunch bags stamped by hand are quick to make and a thoughtful touch on the treat table. Punch two holes in the folded-over top and slip a candy cane through to secure...clever!

Divided ornament boxes with fun, retro art or even flat shirt boxes tied with a sparkly ribbon are perfect for the cookie sampler you'll take home. Great for showing off a few of each variety too!

Vellum bags topped with a vintage-style postcard are easy to assemble ahead of time and make a sweet keepsake after the cookies are gone!

Roll stacks of cookies in colored cellophane and tie at both ends with ribbon...pretty enough to give!

Be sure to keep lots of trimmings on hand...vintage-style buttons, rick-rack, holiday seals, mailing tags and raffia all make the take-home packages extra special.

Fudgy Mint Cheesecake Bars

Refreshing and rich, these are nearly too pretty to eat!

4 1-oz. sqs. unsweetened baking chocolate, coarsely chopped
1/2 c. plus 2 T. butter, divided
2 c. sugar
4 eggs, divided
2 t. vanilla extract
1 c. all-purpose flour
8-oz. pkg. cream cheese, softened
1 T. cornstarch
14-oz. can sweetened condensed milk
1 t. peppermint extract
green food coloring (optional)
1 c. semi-sweet chocolate chips
1/2 c. whipping cream
Garnish: crushed peppermints

Melt baking chocolate with 1/2 cup butter; stir until smooth. Combine chocolate mixture with sugar, 3 eggs, vanilla and flour in a large bowl, blending well. Spread in a greased 13"x9" baking pan. Bake for 12 minutes at 350 degrees. Beat together cream cheese, remaining butter and cornstarch in a medium bowl until fluffy. Gradually beat in condensed milk, remaining egg, peppermint extract and food coloring, if desired. Pour mixture over hot brownie layer; bake for 30 minutes, or until set. Combine chocolate chips and cream in a small saucepan. Cook over low heat until smooth, stirring constantly. Spread over mint layer; let cool. Refrigerate until set; cut into bars. Store covered in refrigerator. Makes 2 to 3 dozen bars.

Christmas Crinkle Cookies

Kris Kringle's favorite!

12-oz. pkg. semi-sweet chocolate chips, divided
1-1/2 c. all-purpose flour
1-1/2 t. baking powder
1/4 t. salt
1 c. sugar
6 T. butter, softened
1-1/2 t. vanilla extract
2 eggs
3/4 c. powdered sugar

Place one cup chocolate chips in a microwave-safe bowl. Microwave on high setting for one minute; stir. Microwave at additional 10-second intervals, stirring until smooth. Cool to room temperature. Combine flour, baking powder and salt in a small bowl; set aside. Blend sugar, butter and vanilla in a large bowl; beat in melted chocolate. Add eggs one at a time, stirring well after each. Gradually beat in flour mixture; stir in remaining chips. Chill just until firm. Shape into 1-1/2 inch balls; roll generously in powdered sugar. Place on ungreased baking sheets. Bake at 350 degrees for 10 to 15 minutes, until sides are set and centers are still slightly soft. Cool on baking sheets 2 minutes; place on wire racks to cool completely. Makes 4 to 5 dozen.

Buckeyes

Rich, peanut-buttery balls dipped in chocolate...they're delicious at the holidays or anytime!

1 lb. creamy peanut butter
1 c. butter, softened
1-1/2 lbs. powdered sugar
12-oz. pkg. semi-sweet chocolate chips
1/3 bar paraffin

Blend together peanut butter, butter and powdered sugar, mixing with hands. Shape into one-inch balls; chill. Melt together chocolate chips and paraffin over hot water in a double boiler. Use a toothpick to dip each ball in chocolate, leaving a small spot uncovered. With the tip of a small knife, smooth over hole left by toothpick. Arrange on wax paper-lined baking sheet. Place in cool area or freezer to set. Makes about 5 to 6 dozen candies.

exchange

White Chocolate-Cranberry Bars

Cut these into pretty little diamonds to make them extra fancy!

2-1/4 c. all-purpose flour
1 t. baking powder
1/2 t. baking soda
1/2 t. salt
2/3 c. brown sugar, packed
1/2 c. sugar
1/2 c. butter, softened
2 eggs
2 t. vanilla extract
1 c. cranberries, coarsely chopped
1 c. chopped walnuts
12-oz. pkg. white chocolate chips, divided
1 T. shortening

Combine first 4 ingredients in a large bowl; mix well and set aside. Combine sugars and butter in another bowl; blend until light and fluffy. Beat in eggs one at a time. Add vanilla; blend well. Gradually add flour mixture; stir just until combined. Stir in berries, nuts and 1-1/2 cups chips. Spread in a greased 13"x9" baking pan. Bake at 350 degrees until golden, 30 to 40 minutes. In a small saucepan over low heat, melt remaining chips and shortening, stirring until smooth. Drizzle over top. Cool completely; cut into bars. Makes 3 dozen bars.

Hint of Mint Biscotti

This fudgy biscotti is just right for dipping in warm cocoa or coffee...mint chips are a cool surprise!

1 c. butter
2 c. sugar
6 eggs
1 T. vanilla extract
5 c. all-purpose flour
1-1/2 c. baking cocoa
2 T. baking powder
12-oz. pkg. mint chocolate chips
2 egg yolks, beaten
12-oz. pkg. semi-sweet chocolate chips

Blend together butter and sugar in a large mixing bowl. Beat in eggs one at a time until smooth; stir in vanilla and set aside. Mix flour, cocoa and baking powder in a separate bowl; add to butter mixture and mix well. Stir in mint chocolate chips. Shape dough into 6 long rolls; place on ungreased baking sheets. Brush with egg yolk. Bake at 400 degrees for 25 minutes; remove from oven and let cool completely. Slice each loaf into one-inch slices; return slices to baking sheets. Reduce heat to 350 degrees; return to oven for an additional 10 minutes. Let cool. Melt semi-sweet chocolate chips; drizzle over cookies. Makes about 4 dozen cookies.

Crispy Rocky Road Bites

Drizzle melted peanut butter chips over the chocolate for another layer of decadence.

24 chocolate graham cracker squares
1/2 c. butter, melted
12-oz. pkg. semi-sweet chocolate chips, divided
1 c. white chocolate chips
1 c. toffee chips
2 c. mini marshmallows

Arrange graham crackers on a jelly-roll pan, sides touching. Pour melted butter evenly over crackers; sprinkle with 1-1/2 cups chocolate chips and white chips. Bake for 8 to 10 minutes at 350 degrees, until butter is absorbed. Using a knife or spatula, spread melted chips over crackers; sprinkle with toffee chips and marshmallows. Return to oven for 3 minutes, or until marshmallows begin to soften. Set aside. Place remaining chocolate chips in a small plastic zipping bag. Microwave on medium setting until chips melt, about 2-1/2 to 3-1/2 minutes. Snip a small hole in one corner of bag; drizzle chocolate over crackers. Let cool for 30 minutes; cut into bars. Makes 4 dozen bars.

Mint Cream Wafers

Delicate with a creamy filling, it's hard to stop at just a few of these!

1-1/2 c. butter, softened and divided
2 c. all-purpose flour
1/3 c. evaporated milk
2 to 3 c. sugar
1 t. vanilla extract
2-1/3 c. powdered sugar
1/4 t. peppermint extract
red and green food coloring
Optional: 2 to 3 T. finely chopped fresh mint, finely crushed peppermint candies

Beat together one cup butter, flour and milk with an electric mixer on medium speed. Form into a ball; chill for 2 hours. Roll out dough 1/8-inch thick on a lightly floured surface; cut with a 1-1/2" round cookie cutter. Press into sugar; place on ungreased baking sheets. Prick each cookie 3 times with a fork. Bake at 375 degrees for 7 to 9 minutes, or until lightly golden. Cool on a wire rack. Beat remaining butter on medium speed for 30 seconds. Add vanilla; gradually add sugar, beating until smooth and creamy. Beat in peppermint extract, if using. Divide mixture into 2 bowls; tint one with red coloring, the other with green. Generously spread bottoms of 1/4 of the cookies with red frosting and 1/4 with green frosting. Lightly sprinkle frosting with snipped mint or crushed candies, if desired. Top with remaining cookies, bottom sides down. Makes about 5-1/2 dozen cookies.

Peanut Butter Fudge

Cut into fun shapes with a mini cookie cutter...stack, wrap in cello and tie with a ribbon for fun!

1 t. cornstarch
1 T. water
1 lb. brown sugar
3 T. sugar
1 T. butter
1/2 c. milk
1 t. vanilla extract
8-oz. jar creamy peanut butter

Combine cornstarch and water; set aside. Stir together sugars, butter and milk in a heavy saucepan over medium heat until sugars dissolve. Continue cooking until mixture reaches the soft ball stage, or 234 to 243 degrees on a candy thermometer. Stir in cornstarch mixture; immediately remove from heat and mix well. Blend in vanilla and peanut butter. Pour into a buttered 8"x8" baking dish. Chill until set. Makes about 2 pounds.

A toast to cookies! Show them off in pressed-glass goblets or stack them up in champagne flutes. Any stemmed glassware will work. For a warm & cozy twist, pile cookies in oversized mugs instead.

APPETIZERS

BEVERAGES

BREADS

BREAKFASTS

COOKIES, BARS & CANDY

DESSERTS

index

MAINS

MISCELLANEOUS

SALADS

SIDES

SOUPS

EXTRAS